JEFFERSON'S CHILDREN

The Story of One American Family

JEFFERSON'S CHILDREN

The Story of One American Family

by SHANNON LANIER *&* JANE FELDMAN
with photographs by Jane Feldman

Introduction by Lucian K. Truscott IV
HISTORICAL ESSAYS BY ANNETTE GORDON-REED *&* BEVERLY GRAY

RANDOM HOUSE • New York

Sources of photographs and other art are cited on pages 142–143.

"Lucian K. Truscott IV" was originally published as "Jefferson's Children" in the July 1999 issue of *Life* magazine.
Copyright © 1999 by Lucian K. Truscott IV. Reprinted by permission of the author.

"Jill Sim" was adapted from an article entitled "Fading to White"
first published in the February/March 1999 issue of *American Heritage* magazine.

www.randomhouse.com/kids

Library of Congress Cataloging-in-Publication Data
Lanier, Shannon.   Jefferson's children : the story of one American family / by Shannon Lanier and Jane Feldman ;
with photographs by Jane Feldman ; and an introduction by Lucian K. Truscott IV.
p.   cm.   Includes index and bibliographical references.
ISBN 0-375-80597-4 (trade) — ISBN 0-375-90597-9 (lib. bdg.)
1. Jefferson, Thomas, 1743–1826—Family—Juvenile literature.   2. Hemings, Sally—Family—Juvenile literature.
3. Jefferson family—Juvenile literature.   4. Hemings family—Juvenile literature.
5. Afro-Americans—Interviews—Juvenile literature.
6. Racially mixed people—United States—Interviews—Juvenile literature.
7. Afro-Americans—Genealogy—Juvenile literature.
8. Racially mixed people—United States—Genealogy—Juvenile literature.
9. United States—Race relations—Juvenile literature.
[1. Jefferson, Thomas, 1743–1826—Family.   2. Hemings, Sally—Family.   3. Jefferson family.   4. Hemings family.
5. Racially mixed people—Interviews.   6. United States—Race relations.]   I. Feldman, Jane.   II. Title.
E332.2.L35   2000   973.4'6'0922—dc21   [B]   00-44551

Printed in the United States of America   September 2000   10 9 8 7 6 5 4 3 2 1

Designed by Sallie Baldwin and Bob Antler

Dedicated to the American Family—

to the ancestors who preceded us,
the families that surround us now,
and the generations to come.

May we someday truly be one American family.

Introduction

BY LUCIAN K. TRUSCOTT IV

Lucian K. Truscott IV with his daughter, Lilly, and wife, Carolyn.

THE BOOK THAT YOU HOLD IN YOUR HANDS gives eloquent testimony in photographs and interviews that Thomas Jefferson had not one but two families. His first family was with his wife, Martha. I am a fifth great-grandson of Thomas Jefferson, through their daughter Martha Jefferson Randolph. After the death of his wife, Thomas Jefferson had a relationship with his slave Sally Hemings and fathered seven of her children. The people you will meet in these pages are descended from these two women.

It's a sad fact that two hundred years after Jefferson's relationship with Sally Hemings was first exposed in a Virginia newspaper, nearly fifty years after the Supreme Court ordered an end to segregated schools and forty years after the civil rights movement ended segregation in the South, there is still resistance to the notion that Mr. Jefferson had children with a slave.

There would seem to be an easy explanation why this is so. Racism—the bald-faced lie that whites are inherently superior to blacks—explains part of it, for if our founding father Thomas Jefferson was superior to his slave Sally Hemings, how could he have a relationship with her? Several generations of historians have indulged in the same kind of reasoning and staked their professional careers on protecting the reputation of Mr. Jefferson from stories that he was guilty of "race mixing."

But these explanations are not enough. The denial of Jefferson's relationship with Sally Hemings is deeply rooted in two hundred years of America's silence about slavery, as if by not talking about it we could wish it away. But three centuries of slavery have not gone away. They are part of a long, hard legacy we as a nation have failed to properly remember and account for. That we find ourselves at this late date confronting our tortured racial past in the person of Thomas Jefferson speaks volumes about how short has been the distance we've come since he wrote "all men are created equal."

It's easy for us as American citizens to turn our heads—to have wealth and ignore poverty, to be healthy and ignore the sick, to be educated and ignore those who cannot read and write, to vote and ignore those striving to become citizens and gain the vote. It's as if our constant forward motion leaves behind us a turbulent wake obscuring our past. Yet we will fail history if all we do is look to the future.

Our racial history in America has been freighted with lies. Much of it has been covered up, and the truth about slavery has been hidden away and denied. Historians have refused to listen to African-American history as it has been passed down through the generations. It should be made clear right here, right now, that the Jefferson/Hemings story has been controversial only among white people. African Americans have long accepted the story, passing it as oral history from one generation to the next.

That is why the story of Thomas Jefferson and Sally Hemings is so important. It shows us that the truth of our racial past has been right before our eyes all along. All we have to do as Americans is to wake up in the morning and go outside. Around us walk people who proudly present to the world their faces in a rich mix of colors. Their pride is all the evidence we'll ever need that race mixing is as American as apple pie, motherhood, and stock car racing.

If we can look at these photographs of Mr. Jefferson's great-grandchildren, we can finally as a nation begin to bridge the gap between his life and his beliefs, a gap that Mr. Jefferson did not bridge when he failed to free his slaves on the day he wrote the Declaration of Independence. If we can finally admit that the third President of the United States had two families, and that one of his families was African-American, then we can demystify race.

All these years since the founding of our country, we have been led to believe by law and culture and ugly racial attitudes that we are separate and different because of the color of our skin. But the story of Thomas Jefferson and Sally Hemings teaches us that we haven't been separate, different families. We have been one family all along.

In the pages of this book, you will meet people from the Martha side of the family, and you will meet people from the Sally side of the family. I am proud to call all of the people in this book my cousins. When I appeared on *The Oprah Winfrey Show* with my sister Mary and twenty-five of our Hemings cousins, I invited them to accompany me to the annual reunion of the Monticello Association, the organization of descendants of Thomas and Martha Jefferson. In 1999, more

Anne Harloe Truscott and Lucian K. Truscott III with their children,
Virginia, Lucian IV, Susan, Mary, and Frank.

Lucian's great-grandparents William Mann and Mary Walker Randolph (right).

Lucian's grandfather Lucian K. Truscott, Jr., with his son James (below right).

than fifty Hemings cousins came to the reunion, and in years ahead, many more will come. I have worked hard to get the Hemings cousins admitted into the Monticello Association, because they, too, are descendants of Thomas Jefferson. After all, Sally Hemings was Martha Jefferson's half sister. When you look at the hidden history of Mr. Jefferson, you find that we are all related one way or another anyway.

In my family, our mom and dad told us Mr. Jefferson meant it when he wrote that "all men are created equal." We were raised as his great-grandchildren, and we were taught to live by and act upon his words. That is what I mean when I say that the story of Thomas Jefferson and Sally Hemings demystifies race. If you accept Mr. Jefferson's words, that we are all created equal, then you accept that we are not separate and different. We are equal.

There is a terror faced by those who would deny the truth in these pages: that one day race will cease to matter, and from that moment on, our hearts will know no boundaries.

As a great-grandson of Thomas Jefferson, my heart knows no boundaries when it comes to my family. We are many, we children of Mr. Jefferson, and we are a family. You will learn in these pages that when he helped to create this nation, he also created a family that looks like America.

This is a book about Mr. Jefferson's family. It is a book about my cousins. I am proud to be the cousin of its author, proud to be one of Jefferson's children.

SWORN UPON
WE HOLD THESE TRUTHS TO BE SELF-
EVIDENT: THAT ALL MEN ARE CREATED
EQUAL, THAT THEY ARE ENDOWED BY THEIR
CREATOR WITH CERTAIN INALIENABLE
RIGHTS, AMONG THESE ARE LIFE, LIBERTY
AND THE PURSUIT OF HAPPINESS, THAT
TO SECURE THESE RIGHTS GOVERNMENTS
ARE INSTITUTED AMONG MEN. WE...
SOLEMNLY PUBLISH AND DECLARE, THAT
THESE COLONIES ARE AND OF RIGHT
OUGHT TO BE FREE AND INDEPENDENT
STATES...AND FOR THE SUPPORT OF THIS
DECLARATION, WITH A FIRM RELIANCE
ON THE PROTECTION OF DIVINE
PROVIDENCE, WE MUTUALLY PLEDGE
OUR LIVES, OUR FORTUNES AND OUR
SACRED HONOUR.
THOMAS JEFFERSON
1743–1828

WE HOLD THESE TRUTHS TO BE SELF-EVIDENT, THAT ALL MEN ARE CREATED EQUAL...

"What exactly did you mean when you wrote those words?"
That's one question I've always wanted to ask
my great-great-great-great-great-great-grandfather
Thomas Jefferson.

My name is Shannon Lanier. I am a twenty-year-old descendant of Thomas Jefferson and his slave Sally Hemings. Madison Hemings, one of their youngest children, was my direct ancestor. How do I know this? Sometimes it feels like I was born knowing. I remember when I was in the first grade, on Presidents' Day, I stood up and told the class I was the sixth great-grandson of Thomas Jefferson. The teacher told me to sit down and quit telling lies. I was so hurt I came home that afternoon and told my mom all about it. The next day, she marched in there and told the teacher that her son wasn't lying. "Where is your proof?" the teacher asked. "Where in the history books does it say that this is so?" And my mom told her that she had learned from her mama as her mama had learned from hers, and so on, from lips to ears, down through the generations.

I believe I inherited much from both sides of my family. From Sally and Madison, I inherited the stories that were handed down—my oral history—and a strong sense of family. From Jefferson, I inherited an insatiable love of learning and a belief that we are all created equal. Although Jefferson was one of the founders of the United States, his family is not yet united, because many of the descendants of Jefferson and his wife, Martha, still refuse to acknowledge as family the descendants of Jefferson and his slave Sally Hemings.

It's always been a dream of mine to come to know my larger family— both the other branches of the Hemings family and the Jefferson side as well. But never in my wildest dreams did I ever think it would be possible.

The Oprah Winfrey Show

I've learned a lot of lessons in my life, but one of the biggest lessons of all I learned on that day in first grade. I learned not to share the knowledge of my lineage with too many people. I mean, why bother? People would just say I was lying. Besides, it was enough that my family and I knew. But in the fall of 1998, all that changed forever.

I was in my dorm room at Kent State University when my mom called. I'll never forget. I was working on an economics paper, and it was really hard, and I was happy to get called away from it.

"Turn on *Oprah*," my mom told me. "Our family is on the show today."

I had already known that something was brewing. Ten days earlier, the news had broken of Dr. Eugene Foster's DNA findings linking Thomas Jefferson to his slave Sally Hemings through Eston, their youngest son. It was one thing to read it in the newspaper. It was another thing to see it validated on national TV. On *Oprah* yet! I ran to the TV and turned it on.

Sure enough, there they were. There were my cousins Shay and Doug sitting right next to Oprah. In the audience I saw my uncle Billy and cousin Patti Jo. And there were a whole bunch of other people I had never seen before in my life. But there was Oprah introducing them as my cousins. There was Lucian Truscott IV and his sister Mary, descendants of Thomas and Martha. Lucian was very vocal. Here was a man who, with his brother, Frank, had played on the grounds at Monticello as a child, and he was actually proud to acknowledge on national TV that he had African-American relatives! I couldn't believe it when, at the end of the show, he boldly invited his Hemings cousins—those on the show and those, like me, who might be watching at home—to come to the annual Jefferson family reunion at Monticello in May.

I practically stood up and cheered. This was it. This was my chance to realize my dream: to actually meet the family I had always known I had. I had so many questions for them. How had they come to know their family stories? How did they feel about being descended from T.J.? How were we alike and how were we different and, most important, would we get along, just because a strand of DNA said we were all related? I couldn't wait to go to the reunion to find out.

Just after taping the <u>Oprah</u> show, Hemingses and Jeffersons sit down for a meal together.

*O*n May 15, 1999, we, the descendants of Martha Jefferson and Sally Hemings, made history standing on the steps of Monticello as one American family. That was the day I first met photographer Jane Feldman. She had come to Monticello to capture on film those who recognize themselves as one family. I ran up and grabbed the microphone. I called the family up to the steps and, sure enough, eighty of us proudly came together for this historic photograph, which later appeared in newspapers and magazines worldwide.

The reunion was amazing. I went around making contact with as many family members as I could. There were Jeffersons there who threw their arms around me, and one woman who looked at my outstretched hand and actually shuddered. There were Hemingses who looked as white as Jeffersons and some who even had the Jefferson name. There were Hemingses who were angry at having to prove our lineage, and there were Jeffersons who absolutely refused to acknowledge the scientific evidence or our oral history. And everywhere there was talk. "Do you think Thomas loved Sally?" "How could a man who preached equality be a slave owner?" "Does anybody have a picture of Sally?" "How did you find out?" "Have you always known?" "How does it feel?" "Are you proud?" "Are you ashamed?" "Was the founding father of our country a hypocrite?" There just wasn't enough time that day to meet everybody and get down and talk to them the way I wanted to, the way I *needed* to. Jane and I decided that day to travel the country and get better acquainted with my family. I left the mountaintop in Virginia knowing that the best way to start my trip was to retrace the footsteps of my ancestor Madison Hemings on the journey he had once made from Virginia to southern Ohio.

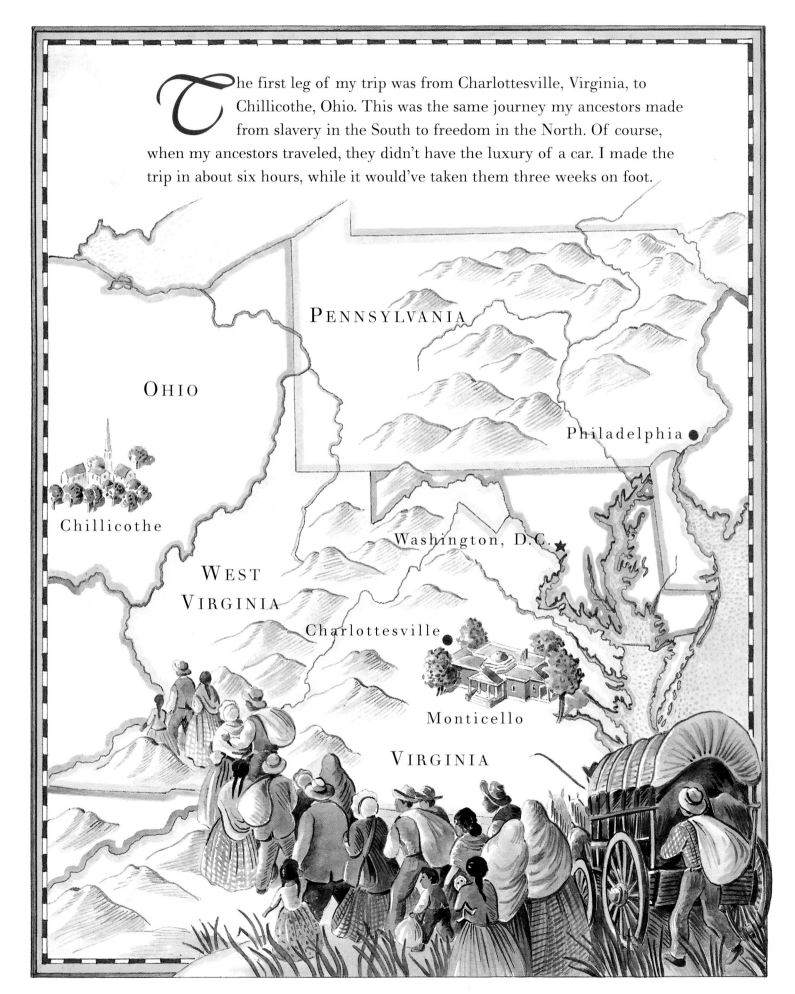

The first leg of my trip was from Charlottesville, Virginia, to Chillicothe, Ohio. This was the same journey my ancestors made from slavery in the South to freedom in the North. Of course, when my ancestors traveled, they didn't have the luxury of a car. I made the trip in about six hours, while it would've taken them three weeks on foot.

PENNSYLVANIA

OHIO

Philadelphia

Chillicothe

Washington, D.C.

WEST VIRGINIA

Charlottesville

Monticello

VIRGINIA

$\mathcal{J}$ust as I knew that the best place to start my journey was Ohio, I knew that the best person to start it with was Beverly Gray. In Chillicothe, my mom and my grandma joined me, and we went to meet Bev, who is the most knowledgeable about our family of anyone we know.

Bev is an oral historian who has spent thirty years researching and preserving the history of all the Monticello slave families—including my family, the Hemingses. Although Bev is not a Hemings, our families have had strong ties ever since my ancestors arrived in Ohio. Bev brings the past to life. She has preserved many written records, including birth and death certificates, family Bibles, and maps, and also helps to preserve oral history through interviews. She helped all three of us find our places in our family tree.

After the interview, Bev took us to see the land Madison once owned, the graveyard where his tombstone was unfortunately destroyed, the grave-site of his daughter Sarah, and my great-great-grandmother Ella's house, which had once been a stop on the Underground Railroad.

Beverly Gray

WHAT I WANT IS FOR ALL CHILDREN, no matter who they are, to be able to celebrate what they are. I'm proud of my black heritage. Young people need to stop being ashamed of being black. They need to know they have a heritage, they have a culture, and they have traditions that are unique to themselves, just like the Irish, the Germans, and others.

No, this is not my family, but it's been my charge to see to it that other people know the story. Now it's up to your generation. Now it's your charge to tell them, to tell somebody else, just as it's been my charge, because a family story is a legacy. It doesn't belong to one person.

Shannon at what is left of his great-great-grandmother Ella's house, once a stop on the Underground Railroad.

It has to be passed on. People ask why it's relevant, and I say because kids don't know who they are anymore.

Look at your ancestor Madison Hemings. He learned how to live as a free person straight out of slavery. That's something people don't understand: If you were a slave, you didn't know what it was like to live as an independent person. Madison learned to make his way. He raised good people—good, hardworking people. For example, Emma, his granddaughter, and her husband, George Young, were farmers, and they were excellent farmers. They owned 435 acres at one time. This was something to be proud of.

Madison was a fourth-generation slave. His mother was a slave, her mother was a slave, and her mother was a slave. So all they knew was slavery. And to think Madison and his brother Eston came six hundred miles north—through the mountains, across major rivers—and settled in an area, carved out farms, built houses, had smokehouses, had barns, planted orchards, and raised families!

People don't understand how hard that was because we have not been allowed to progress at the rate that we ought to. Slavery pulled families apart. They were sold off. They were taken off, and they were prevented from seeing each other. When slavery was over, they went where they could make a living, and this was dispersing. It's almost like the tribes of Israel that were dispersed in the Bible. And then when Israel was formed in 1947 or 1948, the tribes came home again. One of the reasons I think all this is so important is to me it's like coming home again. You come home sometimes as a white person, you come home sometimes as a black person, but it's the coming back together of these groups of people that were once dispersed. And you see this happening, not only with the Jefferson story, but with many, many families, and with all families touched by slavery. And I think that this coming together of family can do more for brotherhood than multicultural diversity can ever do because it's family. And when people learn that they can be a family—even if they're not the same, or don't look alike, or whatever—then the world will be a better place.

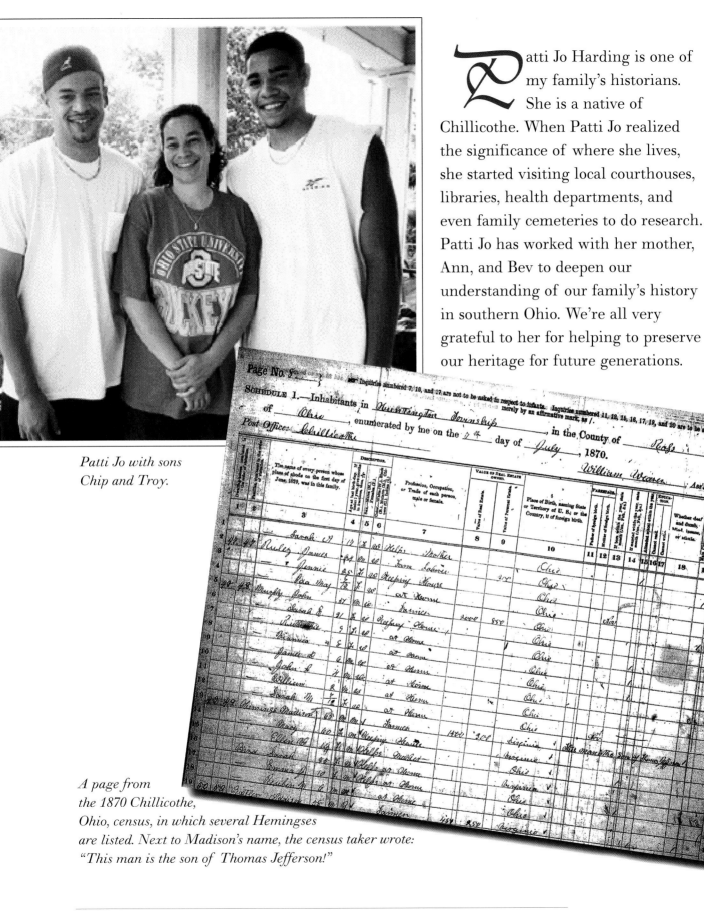

Patti Jo with sons
Chip and Troy.

Patti Jo Harding is one of my family's historians. She is a native of Chillicothe. When Patti Jo realized the significance of where she lives, she started visiting local courthouses, libraries, health departments, and even family cemeteries to do research. Patti Jo has worked with her mother, Ann, and Bev to deepen our understanding of our family's history in southern Ohio. We're all very grateful to her for helping to preserve our heritage for future generations.

A page from
the 1870 Chillicothe,
Ohio, census, in which several Hemingses
are listed. Next to Madison's name, the census taker wrote:
"This man is the son of Thomas Jefferson!"

One of the best ways to learn about the family is to create a family tree. My tree reflects eleven generations going back to my first ancestor in this country, who is referred to as the "Unnamed African Woman." She had a child, whose name was Elizabeth, with Captain John Hemings. Elizabeth and a man named John Wayles had Sally Hemings. John Wayles was also the father of Thomas Jefferson's wife, Martha. That made Sally Hemings and Martha Wayles Jefferson half sisters!

Sally Hemings and Thomas Jefferson had seven children, two of whom died. The second youngest was Madison Hemings.

It's easier if I just show you...

Shannon at the tombstone of Sarah Byrd.

My Family Tree

THIS FAMILY TREE REPRESENTS nine generations of my family, through my mother's side. Bev made me recite all the names in the tree in their proper order, over and over, until I had them memorized. She also made me stop and think about the individuals and who they were. With this understanding, and with the family photos we brought that day, we put together the tree you see here.

Traditionally, a family tree starts with the oldest known ancestors and works forward in time. For me that would have been Sally's grandparents the Unnamed African Woman and Captain John Hemings. But for the sake of clarity, I've started with myself and worked in reverse order back to Thomas Jefferson and Sally Hemings.

As you know, I'm Shannon Lanier.
(B. 1979)

My mother is Priscilla Lanier.
(B. 1952)

Her father was Edward Dalton.
(1923–1990)

His mother was Emma Lee Dalton,
my great-grandmother.
(1905–1990)

Her mother was Ella Cooper.
(1884–1930)

Her mother was Emma Young.
(1859–1940)

NO
KNOWN
PHOTO

Her mother was Sarah Byrd.
(1835–1884)

NO
KNOWN
PHOTO

Her dad was Madison Hemings.
(1805–1877)

His parents were
Thomas Jefferson (1743–1826)
and
Sally Hemings (1773–1835).

We believe that this portrait of my family is dated around 1915. Bev taught me that when photographs are not marked with their dates, you have to judge by the ages of the people and the style of their clothing and their hair. My great-great-great-grandmother Emma and her husband, George Young (seated in the middle), are surrounded by their ten children, including my great-great-grandmother Ella. We know a lot about the ancestors in my direct line from Ella, as well as from her three siblings who chose to identify themselves as black. As was common in those days, many of her siblings passed for white, because it opened many doors. But that often meant cutting ties with their family forever. While this made it possible for future generations to live the American Dream, once they passed, they were lost.

So my family works hard to preserve the parts of our heritage that we have not lost.

This is the family that I was raised knowing. There are four generations of us, and we have always been very close. We get together four or five times a year for family reunions. When we go camping, we sit around the fire and share stories and an extraordinary bond. People marvel at our "rainbow family," but color has never mattered to us. We just love each other.

efore I get too deep into my family story, I'd better back up and talk a little bit about Thomas Jefferson. When I was growing up, the only things we learned in school about T.J. was the stuff everyone knows, like his role in writing the Declaration of Independence and that that was him on the nickel and the two-dollar bill. But because of my connection to him, I did some research on my own and learned some fascinating things. He was an accomplished violinist and architect. He hated public speaking but loved writing. He hated politics but loved the idea of building a nation. He wanted to end slavery but had to give up that fight to get elected President.

To learn more about Jefferson, I went to see an expert, Annette Gordon-Reed, a law professor at New York University and the author of *Thomas Jefferson and Sally Hemings: An American Controversy.*

Thomas Jefferson

BY ANNETTE GORDON-REED

THOMAS JEFFERSON WAS A MAN OF GREAT ACCOMPLISHMENTS and extraordinary contradictions. The catalog of his life achievements—stunning in its breadth and depth—is unmatched by any other figure in American public life. Jefferson was a lawyer, a state legislator, a governor, an ambassador, a secretary of state, a vice president, and the third President of the United States. In addition to all of this, he is also known as the principal author of the Declaration of Independence, which stands today as the charter of American freedom. While leading the nation he helped to create, President Jefferson pointed America westward with the purchase of the Louisiana Territory, which virtually doubled the size of our country. He then sent Meriwether Lewis and William Clark in search of the Northwest Passage to the Pacific Ocean. After retiring from public service, Jefferson devoted his final years to the founding of the University of Virginia. President John Kennedy paid him homage when he described an event honoring a group of Nobel laureates as "the most extraordinary collection of human knowledge gathered together at the White House since Thomas Jefferson dined alone."

For all of his accomplishments, there is one feature of Jefferson's story that has troubled observers from his day until ours. Even though he is considered the principal architect of American freedom, Jefferson was a lifelong owner of slaves. Despite his stated belief—formed in his youth—that slavery was fundamentally evil, Jefferson failed during his lifetime to sever his links to that institution.

Slavery was an integral part of the Virginia society into which Jefferson was born on April 13, 1743. He was, by birth, a member of Virginia's planter elite. His father, Peter, a surveyor, was known for having produced one of the eighteenth century's most accurate maps of Virginia. Jefferson's mother, Jane, was a member of the Randolph family, whose roots in Virginia dated back to the earliest colonial settlers. It is clear, however, that it was the father who had the most influence upon his son. It was his father, Thomas Jefferson said, who instilled in him such a deep love of and respect for books and education. Peter Jefferson made sure that his son received the best education available to a young man in Virginia.

Jefferson pursued his studies with enthusiasm. He learned Greek, Latin, and French, and developed a particular fondness for mathematics. But his world was shattered at age fourteen when Peter Jefferson died. Later, Jefferson would say that his father's death left him feeling absolutely alone in the world. But Peter Jefferson's death transformed Thomas in an even more substantial way. He inherited thirty-five slaves. Because he was a minor, this "property" was under the control of the men who had been appointed his guardians. At the age of twenty-one, Jefferson became a full-fledged master of slaves, a position he was to remain in until his death sixty-two years later.

After completing his primary and secondary education, Jefferson attended the College of William and Mary in Williamsburg, Virginia. He decided to pursue a career in law, studying under George Wythe, a man who would exert a lifelong influence upon him. After passing the bar, Jefferson entered the practice of law, working mainly in the Williamsburg area. It was there that he met the woman who would become his wife, Martha Wayles Skelton, recently widowed with a young son. Jefferson family lore has it that Thomas and Martha were united by their

THOMAS JEFFERSON—TIME LINE

1743	1768	1772	1773
Jefferson born	Construction of Monticello begins	Jefferson marries Martha Wayles Skelton	Sally Hemings born

common love of music. The couple were married in 1772, when Jefferson was twenty-eight and Martha was twenty-three.

Jefferson brought his bride home to what would become one of the most famous residences in the world—Monticello. He began work on his mountaintop

The will and codicil of Thomas Jefferson, in which he freed Madison and Eston Hemings.

1775	1782	1784	1787	1790	1800	1810	1826	1835
Jefferson writes Declaration of Independence	Martha Jefferson dies	Jefferson posted to Paris	Sally joins Jefferson in Paris	Thomas Woodson born	Jefferson elected President	Jefferson retires to Monticello	Jefferson dies	Sally dies

home in Virginia when he was twenty-five. The work never ceased; he persisted in putting up and tearing down sections of the building, revising and renovating it until the time of his death.

Because of his commitment to the goals of the American Revolution and because of what John Adams described as his "felicity of expression," Jefferson was chosen by the Continental Congress to draft the American Declaration of Independence. Although the final version of that document was the work of a committee, Jefferson's own contribution has resonated in the hearts and minds of Americans— and people the world over—as the most eloquent statement in favor of human freedom ever expressed.

While the success of the Revolution brought Jefferson great joy, personal happiness was elusive. In 1782, his beloved wife died from complications due to childbearing. Over the course of their brief ten-year marriage, Martha had given birth to six children, with each pregnancy sapping more and more of her strength. Of the six children born to Thomas and Martha, only two survived to adulthood: Martha—later called Patsy—and Mary—later known as Polly, or Maria. One of Jefferson's sisters described her brother as being prostrate with grief at the loss of Martha. It has been said that Jefferson promised her on her deathbed that he would never marry again.

Jefferson wasn't allowed to indulge his grief for long. In 1784, President George Washington sent him to France as a representative of the new American government. His oldest daughter, Patsy, accompanied him, while his two youngest children, Polly and Lucy, remained in Virginia with their aunt, Elizabeth Eppes. Jefferson also brought along a slave named James Hemings, who was to be trained as a chef. The three Virginians took up residence in the Hôtel de Langeac in a fashionable section of Paris.

The Hemings family had come to Monticello as part of the property that Martha Wayles Jefferson had inherited from her father, John Wayles. The matriarch of the Hemings clan, Elizabeth had been the mistress of John Wayles and had borne him six children. James Hemings, who was one of those children, was the half brother of Jefferson's deceased wife. Matters became even more complicated when James's younger sister, Sally—Martha's half sister—arrived in Paris along with Jefferson's daughter Polly. At some point during the course of their stay in Paris, Jefferson took Sally as his mistress. When they returned to the United States, Sally was pregnant with a child who, according to an interview her son Madison

Hemings gave, lived only a short time. Others say that the child lived and grew up to be Thomas Woodson.

Upon his return to America, Jefferson served in George Washington's Cabinet as the first secretary of state. After a brief period of retirement in the mid-1790s, he became vice president under John Adams. Although his neighbors in Virginia gossiped about his relationship with Sally Hemings, they continued to hold him in high esteem. After Jefferson won the presidency in the election of 1800, James Callender, who had been a Jefferson supporter, turned on him and printed the story of Jefferson and Sally's relationship, hoping to ruin Jefferson's chances for a second term. Callender did not succeed. Jefferson was re-elected to a second term by a landslide.

When Jefferson retired to Monticello in 1810, he quickly became aware that he was in dire financial straits. One of the more puzzling aspects of Jefferson's character is that he was a lifelong record-keeper who kept track of each expenditure and debt down to the penny, yet he habitually lived beyond his means. He also had the bad fortune to be a farmer during a series of severe economic crises in Virginia. By the time of his death, Jefferson was over $100,000 in debt.

Jefferson died on July 4, 1826, on the fiftieth anniversary of the signing of the Declaration of Independence. His death was catastrophic for the slave population at Monticello. Only five slaves were freed by Jefferson's will. Two of them, Madison and Eston Hemings, were his sons with Sally. Their two older siblings, Beverley (a male) and Harriet, had left Monticello several years before Jefferson's death. Sally Hemings went to live with her sons in Charlottesville. The rest of Monticello's slaves were sold at auction, most of them separated from family and friends. Patsy, Jefferson's only surviving daughter with his wife, and her numerous children were left in desperate financial circumstances. Monticello fell out of the hands of the Jefferson family forever.

Despite Jefferson's flaws and contradictions, his legacy is of immense value. To examine his life is to examine the most difficult and challenging aspects of American culture. He was at the center of the birth of this nation. He continues to be at the center of its development as we ponder how we came to be the people we are today.

*U*nfortunately, we know a lot less about Sally Hemings. There are no photographs or paintings of Sally (that we know of), but she was described by fellow slave Isaac as being "mighty near white." She was mulatto, the half sister of Thomas Jefferson's wife, Martha. To get the story of Sally Hemings and her children, I went back to Beverly Gray, whose expertise on the Hemings family is unmatched.

Sally Hemings

BY BEVERLY GRAY

SALLY HEMINGS WAS BORN A SLAVE IN 1773, near Williamsburg, Virginia. Her father, John Wayles, was a lawyer and a slave trader and owned the plantation on which Sally was born. Sally's mother, Elizabeth Hemings, was one of John Wayles's slaves.

The year before Sally's birth, John Wayles's legitimate daughter Martha married Thomas Jefferson. When John Wayles died, Thomas Jefferson inherited his wife's portion of her father's slaves. Betty Hemings and her children were a part of that inheritance. When the Hemings family arrived at Monticello, Martha's half sister Sally was approximately three years old.

Ten years after Martha Wayles married Jefferson, her health began to fail and, after a long illness following childbirth, she died. Present during the last moments of Martha's life were her husband and several of the Hemings slave family, including Sally.

After the death of his wife, the grieving Jefferson went to Europe in the summer of 1784 as the United States Minister to France. Accompanying him were his oldest daughter, Patsy, and his slave James Hemings, the brother of Sally. Jefferson took James to Paris in order to have him learn French cookery, of which Jefferson was extremely fond.

Jefferson did not take his entire family with him, but left his younger daughters, Lucy and Maria, behind in Virginia. A year after Jefferson's arrival in France, he received devastating news of the death of his daughter Lucy. This tragedy spurred him to send for Maria. Fourteen-year-old Sally Hemings was entrusted with the responsibility of accompanying the ten-year-old Maria on the arduous voyage across the ocean and taking care of her in France. Maria and Sally set sail in July 1787, going first to London, where they stopped awhile with John and Abigail Adams. In Paris, Jefferson arranged for Sally to be trained as a lady's maid. She was taught fine sewing and dressmaking, as well as how to dress hair in the fashion of the day. Because Sally was expected to accompany Martha Jefferson when she attended social occasions, appropriate clothing was purchased for her.

A Monsieur Perrault tutored Sally's brother James for a period of twenty months in the French language. Some historians believe that Perrault may have tutored Sally as well. We do know that she learned the language well enough to converse in French with Martha Jefferson and Martha's friends. Sally's son Madison said in an interview with an Ohio newspaper in 1873 that his mother was just beginning to learn French well when she left France.

Slavery was illegal in France and so, while she was on French soil, Sally was not technically a slave. She was paid regular wages from the fall of 1788 until she returned to the United States in 1789. Her salary was the equivalent of $2.00 a month, an amount much less than most French servants were paid but, nevertheless, an indication of Sally's free status while in France.

Madison said that at this time a relationship developed between his mother and Thomas Jefferson—whom Madison in his

MULBERRY ROW

This 1,000-foot-long road was the center of plantation activity at Monticello from the 1770s until Jefferson's death in 1826. It once was lined with the dependencies necessary to support the main house and a 5,000-acre plantation with as many as 150 residents. In 1796 there were seventeen structures on Mulberry Row, including dwellings for white and black workmen, wood and ironworking shops, a smokehouse-dairy, a wash house, storehouses, and a stable. The diagram below is based on a drawing by Jefferson from 1796.

The grandchildren of Jefferson and Hemings who represent the three lines of the family that can be traced.

A son of Eston Hemings: Beverly Frederick Jefferson.

A son of Thomas Woodson: Lewis Woodson.

A daughter of Madison Hemings: Harriet Butler Spears.

writings referred to as "Father"—and that Sally became pregnant sometime in late 1789. As long as she remained in France, Sally was a free person and the child she was expecting would be born free. James Hemings, who had become an excellent French chef, was free as well. Even so, Jefferson convinced them both to return to America—and to slavery—by promising that any children born to Sally would be freed at age twenty-one. He also promised that she and her brother James would be treated favorably.

Sixteen-year-old Sally returned to Monticello as a maid to eleven-year-old Maria. While Sally may have lived with her mother immediately after her return, she eventually lived in the weaver's cottage at the head of Mulberry Row, the path along which the slaves lived. She then moved farther down Mulberry Row and lived in one of the cabins built for slaves. After the south dependency—a covered row of rooms attached to the main house—was finished in about 1801, Sally moved into a room there, near the all-weather passageway that separates the wings of the house. Sally was responsible for Jefferson's room and his wardrobe. In addition, she did the fine needlework on the dresses of Jefferson's granddaughters.

According to the Thomas C. Woodson family history, it was soon after her return from France that Sally gave birth to a son she named Thomas Jefferson Hemings. In 1802, journalist James Thompson Callender published articles about a slave boy at Monticello who looked so much like Jefferson that it caused local gossip. When Jefferson's political enemies got wind, they made up songs about the slave children of Sally Hemings. Two of these ballads were "Long Tom" and "Dusky Sally."

Woodson family history has it that someone at Monticello arranged for young Thomas—who by then was quite tall and did strikingly resemble Jefferson—to live on another farm. The owner of the plantation was a man named Woodson. Thomas took the name Thomas C. Woodson. He married Jemima Price, a slave on the Woodson farm, and, after purchasing Jemima and their children's freedom, moved to Chillicothe, Ohio. He and Jemima kept themselves apart from the townspeople, but were much respected. They were part of a group of free people of color who left the white Methodist Church and formed the Quinn Chapel African Methodist Episcopal Church in 1821. In 1828, the family moved to Jackson County, Ohio, where they built a home on land they had bought.

The Woodsons raised a family of eleven well-educated children, who served the community in a variety of ways. They were ministers, educators, writers, lecturers, entrepreneurs, barbers, and farmers. Two of their sons were active in the antislavery and anti-colonization movements in southern Ohio, where their activities on the Underground Railroad eventually led to their deaths.

Sally Hemings and Thomas Jefferson had at least four other children. They were Beverley (a son), Harriet, Madison, and Eston. Beverley and Harriet both gained their freedom by being permitted to "run away." Eston and Madison were both freed by Jefferson's will after his death in 1826. The will required that both men serve an apprenticeship for one year with their uncle, John Hemings, who was an accomplished carpenter. This would enable them to have a trade that they could employ as free men in order to provide for their families.

When she was twenty-one years old, Harriet Hemings was given fifty dollars and put on a stagecoach bound for Philadelphia. There she passed into the white world. Madison said that Harriet married well and lived in Washington City (now Washington, D.C.). She bore several children, who never knew of their African ancestry. Madison apparently had news of her until the Civil War; however, he never revealed her identity.

Beverley Hemings was twenty-four when he left Monticello, and according to Jefferson's granddaughter, he was "white enough to pass for white." He went to Washington City and then to Maryland, where he married a white woman. He and his wife had one child, a daughter, who apparently never knew of her ancestry. According to Madison, Beverley's wife was from a very good family.

As free men, Madison and Eston made their home near Monticello in Charlottesville, with their mother, Sally. How Sally obtained her freedom is still debated. She was listed as a part of the slave inventory of the estate of Thomas Jefferson in 1827. It is likely she was freed sometime around 1829, because she appears as a free person on the 1830 census for Virginia along with her two sons and their families. She was also listed as white. Sally's name appears on a special state census taken in 1833 in Virginia as a free person of color.

Madison married Mary Hughes McCoy, a freeborn woman of color, while Eston married Julia Isaacs West, the daughter of a well-to-do Charlottesville mulatto and a Jewish storekeeper. After their mother's death in 1835, Sally's sons sold their property and moved to Ohio.

Madison settled in Pike County, Ohio, where he worked as a farmer and a carpenter. He lived there for nearly twenty years before building his own home in the picturesque hills of Huntington Township in Ross County, Ohio. He did some reconstruction work on a building in Pike County, helping to convert it from a store to a hotel. This building still stands and is called the Emmitt House.

Records show that Madison was about five feet ten inches tall, lean, with a sandy complexion and light gray eyes. S. F. Wetmore, an Ohio journalist, described him as very intelligent and at ease with himself. Like Eston, he was a musician and, according to ex-slave Isaac Jefferson, a very fine one. In his community, he was known as an honest businessman. A family named Malone lived near Madison and sold seed corn to him. The Malone family oral tradition states that Madison's word was his bond, and that no written receipt was ever needed when dealing with him. His relationship to Thomas Jefferson was widely accepted by his neighbors. In fact, some went so far as to call him "junior president." Madison and Mary had nine children. Only one passed into the white world. Many of the others stayed in Ohio, where their descendants still live today.

Madison's oldest child, Sarah, married Reuben Byrd in 1858. Harriet Hemings married James Butler and lived in Bloomingburg in Fayette County, Ohio.

According to a granddaughter of Ellen Wayles Hemings, shortly before his death Madison arranged a marriage between Ellen and a schoolteacher, Andrew J. Roberts. After the marriage, the Roberts family moved from Ohio to California, where they opened Roberts Funeral Home and were owners of considerable property. Their son was the first person of color ever to serve in the legislature of the state of California.

Two of Madison's sons served in the Civil War. In 1864, sixteen-year-old William Beverly joined the Ohio 73rd OVI Company H, from Chillicothe. He applied for pension after release from service, indicating that he sustained some sort of injury. The other son, Thomas Eston, died of starvation in the notorious Andersonville Prison.

Madison gave his daughter Mary Ann Hemings several articles that had been given to him by his mother, Sally. The items were an inkwell, a pair of spectacles, and a silver buckle, all of which had once belonged to Thomas Jefferson.

Although he was a carpenter by trade, Madison's brother Eston made his living as a violinist in Chillicothe, Ohio. Eston was described as being a remarkably fine-looking colored man. He was six feet tall and light bronze in color, with straight auburn hair and a smattering of freckles on his face. Known as an accomplished musician, he was decidedly intelligent. Some of his neighbors compared his profile to a bronze likeness of Thomas Jefferson. When told of the striking resemblance, Eston said, "Well, my mother, whose name I bear, belonged to Mr. Jefferson, and she never married."

Eston and Julia Hemings sold their property in 1852, then moved to Madison, Wisconsin. Eston changed his name to E. H. Jefferson, and the family made the transition into the white world. Eston and Julia had three children. Their third child, Beverly Hemings Jefferson, was fourteen when the family moved to Wisconsin and changed the family name. He became a respected entrepreneur, owning two hotels and a fleet of omnibuses. Beverly invented a heating apparatus that helped heat the omnibuses, an important feature in this cold climate. His brother John Wayles Hemings Jefferson became a banker, an exporter of cotton, and owner of a cotton company. He died a wealthy man.

Many questions linger about Sally Hemings. What is known as fact is that she was a slave and that she was owned by Thomas Jefferson. The beautiful Sally Hemings enjoyed experiences rarely afforded a slave. She traveled, learned a second language, apparently could read and write, and was given specialized training. She bartered freedom for her children and died a free woman. Unfortunately, because Sally lived most of her life as a slave, what she thought, felt, and valued was not recorded—except through the stories handed down by her descendants from generation to generation.

After learning about my ancestor Madison's line, I thought it was important to learn about the other lines of the Hemings family. In Philadelphia, I visited the descendants of Madison's older brother Tom. Byron Woodson and his wife, Trena, whom I first met at Monticello, maintain and distribute *The Woodson Source Book*. A six-hundred-and-twenty-five-page document, it is a comprehensive recorded history. *The Woodson Source Book* was compiled by Byron's mother, Minnie Woodson. Not only is the book of great use to the family, but many historians have used it as well.

Byron Woodson

MY GRANDFATHER INSPIRED MY MOTHER, MINNIE WOODSON, to get interested in our family history. My grandfather was a very successful man. The high school in the neighborhood where I grew up was named after him, and my mother was always curious about how he got to be so determined and successful. He was an only child and his father died early. So where did he get this ambition? Then there was also the fact that we'd heard we were related to Thomas Jefferson, but we weren't quite sure how. This, of course, would be something different.

The other thing that motivated Mom's research was the fact that all of us feel something about race. My mother felt a lot of pain. She always wondered, "Why is there all this hatred?" That was her perspective. So she put all her energy into her research. My mother was born in 1921, so she would've been fifty-one or fifty-two when she started working on *The Woodson Source Book*. Most of the work was done within a four-year period. My mother's research was voluminous. She compiled the first source book in 1976. It grew from 191 pages to 625. It's amazing to think of this in retrospect. She did all this before personal computers came out. Today you get on the Internet and you can do four years' worth of work in a couple of months.

My mother started her digging in Ohio, with the archives and census data. Then—lo and behold!—along comes Fawn Brodie's book *Thomas Jefferson: An Intimate History*. That was like a lightning rod. She read the book and was actually in touch with her.

Byron and his wife, Trena.

In 1977, the *Washington Post* interviewed us, and I remember Mom saying that she wanted to either prove or disprove the Woodson oral history. She wasn't necessarily stuck on proving the Jefferson connection, she just wanted the truth, but the more research she did, the more she was convinced. When I saw her lay out all of the family photos, the resemblances were impossible to deny.

Tom Woodson and his wife, Jemima, had eleven children, and most of those folks had children. I'm descended from Lewis, their oldest child, and he had twelve children. So after a few generations of that, you've got a lot of folks. The Woodson Association has a membership of fifteen hundred family members. We have yearly reunions. The first reunion was in Pittsburgh in 1976. When we first

Caroline and Lewis Woodson (son of Thomas). They had twelve children.
Pictured below is one of their sons, James, and his wife, Anna Bird Moles.

went to Pittsburgh, probably 85 percent of the people were descended from Lewis, like me—just that one line. But as we went along and got more and more information, the other lines also got connected. This year, for the first time, the descendants of Madison and Eston Hemings will also join the Woodsons' reunion. We are a growing family association and have so much to be proud of.

*R*obert H. Cooley III was a prominent attorney in Petersburg, Virginia, who headed the Thomas Woodson Family Association. Mr. Cooley was a national spokesperson for the family's efforts to prove their kinship to Thomas Jefferson. His work was noted in numerous national magazines and on many network television news shows. He also appeared in Ken Burns's PBS documentary *Thomas Jefferson*. Mr. Cooley attended law school at Howard University, where he was editor-in-chief of the *Howard Law Review* in his first year. After graduation, Mr. Cooley enlisted in the army as a private working in counterintelligence and was commissioned as an officer in 1964. He later practiced law at the Pentagon and was a military judge. Mr. Cooley served in the Army Reserves and retired after twenty years with the rank of lieutenant colonel. His other accomplishments include opening a practice with his father, Robert H. Cooley, Jr.; being appointed the first black magistrate of the U.S. District Court for the Eastern District of Virginia; and helping to establish the first racially integrated law firm in Petersburg.

His dying wish, as a proud descendant of Thomas Woodson, was to be buried in the Monticello graveyard, a request that was denied. The incident started the dialogue as to whether or not Hemingses should be accepted as legitimate descendants of Thomas Jefferson. He is survived by his wife of thirty-six years, Ruby Jean, and his three children, Lisa, Michele, and Robert. Of the three offspring, Michele is the most outspoken in her quest to carry out her father's final wish.

Robert H. Cooley III

July 27, 1939–July 20, 1998

D̲r. Michele Cooley Quille is the daughter of Robert H. Cooley III and an assistant professor at Johns Hopkins University. She attended the May 1999 Monticello Association meeting to represent her father, who died suddenly on July 20, 1998. Michele contributed much to the dialogue at the meeting that weekend and continues to be an active spokesperson for the family.

Michele Cooley Quille

IN 1992, MY FATHER, ROBERT COOLEY, stood up before eleven Virginia historians at a University of Virginia conference and proclaimed, "It's no story. I am a living descendant of Sally Hemings and Thomas Jefferson." Not a single one of them called Daddy a liar. He knew more about what he was talking about than they did. They couldn't refute him. Not one person there said, "Shut up and sit down. You don't know what you're talking about." You would expect someone to challenge what he was saying. Even after the seminar, nobody even wrote or called or said anything to refute his claim.

Daddy had always known who he was. When he was ten, he was told the "family secret." The "family secret" is how it was referred to, because by revealing it, you opened yourself up for denigration and attack by skeptics.

Daddy's death was completely unexpected. Two weeks before he died, he said on national television that he wanted to be buried at Monticello. Daddy died on a Monday. Tuesday, I called the Monticello Association. I told them that Daddy died. I spoke to Robert Gillespie, the president of the Monticello Association at that time, and requested that Daddy be buried there. A day and a half later—which when you're planning a funeral is a long time—Gillespie got back to me with this obviously rehearsed response, saying, "No." He said, "Well, the DNA evidence isn't in." I said, "But what if it *were* in?" He said, "Well, even if it were in, we would have to have more discussions about it. We're not prepared to admit Hemings descendants." And I said, "So you're denying my dad's last request, is that what you're telling me?" And he said, "Yes." Gillespie probably thought that was the end of that.

Jennifer and Robert Cooley IV with his mother, Ruby, and sister Michele.

Michele with baby Alicia.

But Daddy reignited discussions and brought the Hemings/Jefferson issue to the nation's attention. If his death served as a catalyst, I think he's smiling from heaven about it. You talk about spirituality! I pray before discussing anything about this issue. I know that in the end—and I don't know when that end will be—Daddy's mission and his quest will be successful. I think his support is even stronger now that he's in heaven. Daddy had always said, "One of the people that I want to talk to for a long time when I get to heaven is Thomas Jefferson because I have a lot of issues with him!"

Our parents raised us with a sense of pride in our heritage, in our country, and in justice. My grandfather was a prominent civil rights lawyer and my daddy was a lawyer, my uncle is a lawyer, and my aunt is a lawyer. Justice is something that we take very seriously, and inequity is not acceptable. We used to go on lots of family trips. We've been everywhere. My parents have exposed us to a lot of this country and many other countries as well. If Daddy saw something that related to history, we had to check it out. As kids, we would act bored, like "Do we *have* to go to Gettysburg?" But secretly, I enjoyed it. It gave us a sense of how important an understanding of history is. I know I get that from Daddy.

I think it's important that American youth especially get the message: Don't take things for granted and don't take them at face value. Investigate your-self and know who you are because that gives you a sense of strength that no one can take away from you. If you have 100 percent certainty about who you are, you feel secure and you also feel a sense of responsibility for others. We've been a very blessed family, and with those blessings comes responsibility. Even though it's tiresome, even though you have work to do, you take time out to help other people grow. That's what I tell people. I say, "I don't get anything out of this. Nothing tangible. There's no money. I don't get paid for it. I don't get professional develop-ment. I don't get tenure." What do I get out of this? This is something I'm doing for others so that they can understand truth. It's about healing our country. And not just our country but the world.

The real victory has been that we began a dialogue, and that's how you break stereotypes. That's how you end animosity, by sharing ideas and sharing commonalities. You find out how similar we are and that we have a common goal.

I also think, for Shannon's generation, that you need to recognize that just being against the system doesn't do anything. You have to first learn the system and then work within it. I choose to work within systems rather than against

Ruby Cooley with her daughters, Lisa and Michele.

them. If you don't like the way something is, don't just sit on your butt and talk about it. You have to work to change it. Even though it's exhausting, you get such fulfillment from that, because hard work breeds self-confidence and esteem.

That's why the DNA stuff doesn't worry me, because we know who we are. Dr. Eugene Foster contacted my dad when Daddy was the president of the Woodson Association and said, "We want to do some DNA testing to find out whether Jefferson had relations with Sally Hemings that resulted in children. So we need male-line descendants, and I'm asking your help in obtaining them."

Well, Daddy later wrote back to Dr. Foster, saying, "This is something our family needs to think about." Daddy consulted with the Woodson Association board and we opposed it because when we asked for certain assurances, they wouldn't give them. We wanted the blood samples to be independently tested. We wanted our own geneticist to at least peruse and review the tests for accuracy. But they circumvented the Woodson Association and had a genealogist find certain people who said they were male-line descendants of Thomas Jefferson through Thomas Woodson. And that's how they got the blood, much to the opposition of the association.

We know five people volunteered. But who knows? Out of fifteen hundred Woodson family members, five were chosen. We can't even vouch for the people who volunteered, especially since their identities are being kept secret.

As a researcher and a scientist, I understand that you have certain biases. You can manipulate. And you are biased by who is involved and who the funding agency is. I'm not disputing their integrity. I'm disputing who's involved and what controls have been placed. I can't vouch for the entire study. I just can't. But look who was positive. Eston's line. Eston was one of the last kids. Eston comes when Jefferson was an old man and totally out of political office, after he had finished doing most of his major writing. So we can go around and around about what Dr. Foster's team's motivations might have been, and I can't say that the test's not accurate. If they had taken DNA from my brother, then I would believe it as representing me, but they didn't. The point is, *we know who we are.*

*T*hree months after Robert Cooley's death, Dr. Eugene Foster's DNA findings were published. Dr. Foster, a physician and pathologist, had conducted a DNA study that—in connection with historical information—concluded that Eston Hemings, Madison's younger brother, was very probably the son of Thomas and Sally. Finally, there was scientific proof of my family's oral history. Dr. Foster is now retired and living in Charlottesville, Virginia, where I visited him to learn more.

Dr. Eugene Foster

WHAT DOES IT MEAN TO BE A DESCENDANT OF THOMAS JEFFERSON? If you look at it from the genetic standpoint, we're talking now about fifth- to ninth-generation descendants. If you're a fifth-generation descendant, one thirty-second of your DNA came from Thomas Jefferson. With each successive generation, it gets cut in half: one sixty-fourth, one one-hundred-twenty-eighth, one two-hundred-fifty-sixth, and so on. Then you have to ask whether complex behaviors that we believe make the differences between people are determined genetically. There are very few scientists who would say that intelligence, morality, and personality are entirely determined by DNA. But even if you assume that these traits are *entirely* determined by genes, the chances are that the way you act, how you shape your life, and what sort of person you are have practically nothing to do with the genes that you might have gotten from Jefferson.

So what does this ancestry business mean? Does it mean that there is no effect from being descended from some illustrious remote ancestor? I think there is an effect. I think that if you grow up with the belief that you are a descendant of whomever you admire, then that will have shaped your cultural heritage, your attitudes, and many other things about your life. I think that's the case with the Woodson family. They know that they are descendants of Thomas Woodson— Sally and Thomas's first child—maybe not biologically, but it doesn't matter, because they're certainly spiritually and intellectually related to him. That's much of what makes them who they are. If you look at the distinction that so many people in that family have earned, you have to believe that some of it came about

Dr. Foster and his wife, Jane.

because they *believed* that they were descended from Thomas Jefferson and Sally Hemings. And I think that's also true of the Madison Hemings descendants. It's not quite as true of the Eston descendants, because they haven't had this belief for as long a time. That's the funny part. It's ironic that the ones who have the clearest biological link have the least link otherwise.

Look at the present members of the Monticello Association, who are supposed to be descendants of Martha and Maria Jefferson. Not a single one of them has been genetically proven to descend from Thomas Jefferson. Who can believe that there has been no illegitimacy or no adoption in that whole line? Now, if it then gets proved through genetic testing that some of these people are really not descended from Jefferson, what should be their status?

I think that one of the things that all the progress in DNA technology is going to show is that, of course, everybody is related to everybody. We share 99.9 percent of all our DNA; it's the same from one person to the next throughout the world. So, sure we're related. And we're also related to worms! And everything else! That's why this biological aspect of the story to me is the least important. It's classical science—every answer opens more questions than it answers.

I think what has happened is that we have been discussing racial issues we have not talked about very much before. I think it's a wonderful thing, and I'm very pleased with the results.

Tracking the Jefferson Y Chromosome

Only males carry the Y chromosome. All direct descendants in a line share the same or nearly the same Y chromosome. Here's how the match was made.

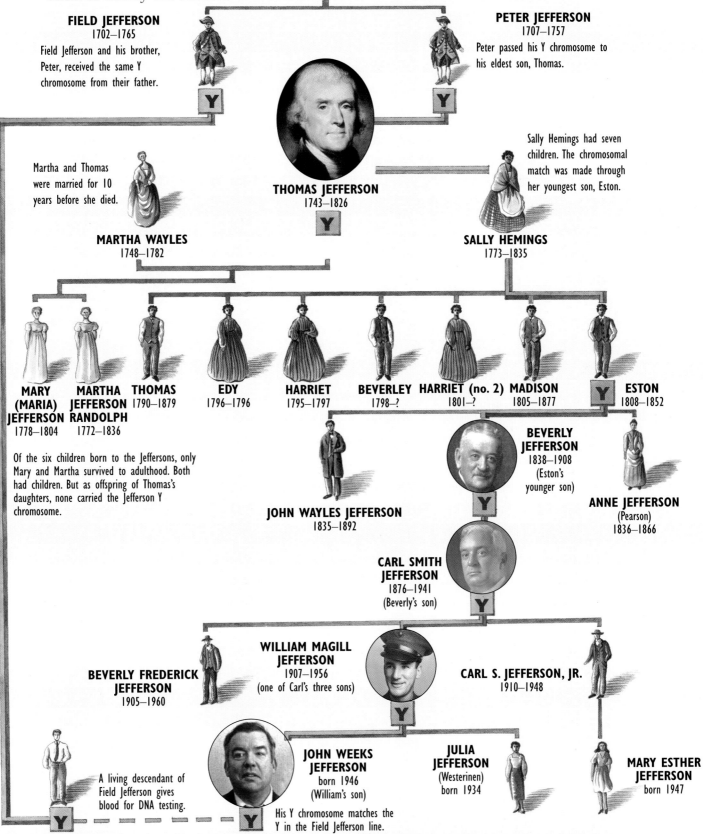

FIELD JEFFERSON
1702–1765

Field Jefferson and his brother, Peter, received the same Y chromosome from their father.

PETER JEFFERSON
1707–1757

Peter passed his Y chromosome to his eldest son, Thomas.

THOMAS JEFFERSON
1743–1826

Martha and Thomas were married for 10 years before she died.

Sally Hemings had seven children. The chromosomal match was made through her youngest son, Eston.

MARTHA WAYLES
1748–1782

SALLY HEMINGS
1773–1835

MARY (MARIA) JEFFERSON
1778–1804

MARTHA JEFFERSON RANDOLPH
1772–1836

THOMAS
1790–1879

EDY
1796–1796

HARRIET
1795–1797

BEVERLEY
1798–?

HARRIET (no. 2)
1801–?

MADISON
1805–1877

ESTON
1808–1852

Of the six children born to the Jeffersons, only Mary and Martha survived to adulthood. Both had children. But as offspring of Thomas's daughters, none carried the Jefferson Y chromosome.

JOHN WAYLES JEFFERSON
1835–1892

BEVERLY JEFFERSON
1838–1908
(Eston's younger son)

ANNE JEFFERSON
(Pearson)
1836–1866

CARL SMITH JEFFERSON
1876–1941
(Beverly's son)

BEVERLY FREDERICK JEFFERSON
1905–1960

WILLIAM MAGILL JEFFERSON
1907–1956
(one of Carl's three sons)

CARL S. JEFFERSON, JR.
1910–1948

A living descendant of Field Jefferson gives blood for DNA testing.

JOHN WEEKS JEFFERSON
born 1946
(William's son)

His Y chromosome matches the Y in the Field Jefferson line.

JULIA JEFFERSON
(Westerinen)
born 1934

MARY ESTHER JEFFERSON
born 1947

Not everyone agrees with Dr. Foster's conclusions. Mr. Barger is a Jefferson family historian of twenty-five years and a retired air force master sergeant. It is his wife, Evelyn, who is the Jefferson. They are not members of the Monticello Association, as it recognizes only direct descendants of Thomas and his wife's daughters, Martha and Maria. Evelyn comes down through the line of Thomas's uncle, Field Jefferson—the same line that provided Jefferson blood for Dr. Foster's test. While I was interviewing him, Mr. Barger told me that he had spent eighteen months researching the burial site of my ancestor William Hemings, Madison's son, and was seeking permission of my family to exhume his body for further DNA testing.

Herbert Barger

I DON'T DISPUTE ANY DNA. I believe the DNA [link to the Jefferson family] is correct. [Linking the DNA to Thomas himself is] the interpretation by Dr. Foster and people in the media, and they're very careful to say "DNA taken in conjunction with historical information." But the fact is [the father] could have been any one of eight Jeffersons, including Thomas.

Anyhow, this whole thing has been blown out of proportion, and the media is making hay out of it. The worst part is we have historical revisionists. Sorry to say, our research—mine and some other people's—indicates that they are pushing the slavery issue. You know, they're piling it all on Jefferson. He was only one slave owner. That was the thing of the time. From everything I read, he was very good to his slaves. I think people have agendas to indoctrinate the American public in the fact that slavery was bad, that Jefferson did do this—we've got science to prove it—but we've got to twist it a little bit to get it there. They're making him out to be a hypocrite. After all, he would be if he said there should be no mixing of the bloods. Now, if he did it, he's a hypocrite, right? What's the next step? Take his head off the nickel? If we could, erase him off of Rushmore?

I'm a man who was on the inside of this study who knows the truth, and I'm trying to tell you, please don't say that Thomas Jefferson fathered any Hemings child. My long history proves he never fa-thered any Hemings child—well, this is my personal opinion based on my over-twenty-five-year study.

We know from the historical and the DNA data that Thomas Jef-ferson can be neither definitely excluded nor solely implicated in the paternity of illegitimate chil-dren with his slave Sally Hem-ings. The simple fact is that the DNA eliminated a long-held be-lief in the oral history of the Woodson family that they were grandchildren of Thomas Jefferson by having no match between Jefferson and Woodson. The Carr brothers were also eliminated by no match. Now, there was *some* Jefferson/Eston Hemings match—just *some*, not Thomas. So in the absence of any other Jefferson to suspect, guess who is left to blame: TOM.

When in fact it could have been any one of eight Jeffersons, including Thomas. The other seven include Thomas's brother, Randolf, one of Randolf's five sons, or George Jr.—Thomas's first cousin once removed.

I encourage the media to come forth and gather the facts and present them to a most deserving public. I will be happy to provide more information if de-sired. I am sure "Old Tom" would thank you, and I know I would. Our children's history must not be tarnished with inaccurate, misleading, and incomplete infor-mation. Thomas Jefferson must not be branded a hypocrite and called other derogatory names just because all the information was not considered in a scien-tific study.

I vigorously oppose the official Thomas Jefferson Memorial Foundation finding, believing it to be incomplete and inaccurate in some of its interpreta-tions. I suggest that a reevaluation of the study be undertaken by impartial re-searchers not associated with the Thomas Jefferson Memorial Foundation.

*J*ulia Jefferson Westerinen and her family have the Jefferson name. They even look like Jeffersons. But the truth is that they are also my Hemings cousins through the Eston line— they were the link in Dr. Foster's DNA study. We met originally at the Monticello Association's annual meeting in May, where there was a historic discussion about whether to accept the Hemings descendants into the association. The association exists solely to care for the Jefferson family graveyard and grant burial. Although at that meeting the Hemingses were not accepted into the association, the discussion continues.

The Westerinens

JULIA: I was told we were related to Jefferson's uncle; that's what was handed down in the family. I don't know who started that lie.

DOROTHY: We knew that we were related to T.J. somehow, but I never heard of Sally Hemings. We were raised believing we were white.

JULIA: It was 1975, after Fawn Brodie's *Thomas Jefferson: An Intimate History* came out. My aunt recognized Eston's name from our family tree and she called the author. Fawn did the research, came east and interviewed us, and said, "You're directly descended from Thomas Jefferson, but through this woman named Sally Hemings, who was his slave." So that's when we first found out about it. Fawn was pivotal. Without her we would not have known any of this. People ask me how it feels, but I'm still finding out. It's a learning, evolving process. I don't know how it feels. It's both wonderful and sad to think Thomas and Sally were never able to say anything about their thirty-eight-year relationship.

DOROTHY: We don't have any of the Hemings oral history. Whether they intended to or not, our ancestors stole it from us. *Somebody* stole it from us. We're just learning—from some of our cousins—stories we weren't able to hear.

MARSHALL: For us it's interesting because, culturally, we're white. We were brought up in a white family as white people. And then, to suddenly find out that you're also descended from slaves....

DOROTHY: And thinking about Sally Hemings and what her life must have been like, that's been a big thought to try and wrap your mind around.

JULIA: Then the *Washington Post* got hold of the story and came up and photographed me, and Lucille Roberts Balthazar in California, who recently passed away, and we made the front page. That was 1976. My son Jeff was twenty-one, Dorothy was nineteen, Art was fifteen, and Marshall was thirteen. It went around the circuit, and then it died.

EMIL: Remember, the historians were still pooh-poohing the idea until the DNA proof came out recently, which was twenty-one years later.

JULIA: Dr. Eugene Foster called my son Art and asked him if anybody in his family would give blood. He needed a male, and Art was willing, but unfortunately it required a direct male line, which was interrupted by me, a female. So we gave Dr. Foster my brother John's phone number. Dr. Foster called John and he went up and took blood, and we forgot about it again. Then the phone rings, and it's *U.S. News & World Report* saying that they wanted to come and interview us. We said, "For what?" They said, "You haven't heard the news?" We said, "No." They said, "The DNA came out positive." Well, I got chills all over. It was just awesome.

DOROTHY: The press went wild.

MARSHALL: Dorothy even got her picture in *Time* magazine. The guy said he wanted to give her a lifetime membership to the NAACP.

JULIA: The media asked me if this had changed my life and I said, "No, not at all." Well, I lied. It changed my life totally. It gave me a new direction, a new career at age sixty-five, doing speaking engagements with my cousin Shay, a new family; a whole new understanding on a gut level, not just intellectual. I was always a liberal intellectual, but now I'm liberal from my toes to the top. You know, I've had my family tree for ages, back to Scotland and England, back to Charlemagne. I didn't think anything of it. A family tree didn't mean anything to me. But it's beginning to mean more.

Since *Oprah*, my reception into the Hemings family has been very generous. I'm just so in love with my new family. They've been wonderful. If I were them, *I* would be very resentful of us, living as privileged because I'm white. I didn't realize I had lived that way. I thought I lived a normal life like everybody else, but that's not true. We walk into a place and of course we're served, we're seated.

DOROTHY: However, that wasn't the case last May at the association meeting. The people who did not want to talk to us and were angry about our presence did not approach us. There were a couple of people who came over in a tentative way and were friendly. I think we kind of fooled them, too, because we were white. They probably assumed we were legitimate members since we had on name tags that said "Monticello Association." But I wrote on mine "Eston Hemings," because I wanted them to know. There were others who came up and said, "We're so glad this has happened. We think it should have happened long ago."

JULIA: I think they have to let us in eventually. I want them to get to know us. We're a great group. In general, I would never join a society like that. I'm not a joiner. I don't join anything, but this one I want in because the principle is important.

DOROTHY: Yeah, it's the principle of the thing. People at my own table stood up to vote against our being in that meeting. They stood right up in our faces. It felt like a blow to my stomach.

MARSHALL: I got glared at a couple times from across the room. It was like

MaryAnn, Dorothy, Emil, Julia, Marshall, Emily, Art, and Susan (left).

Julia's grandmother Esther Jefferson with her sons, Beverly, William, and Carl, Jr. (bottom left).

Julia and her cousin Shay Banks-Young.

Eston descendants at the Jefferson gravesite.

us and them. We have to be careful because we're saying "us" and "them" and that's unfortunate. The ones that characterize the association are the loudest ones, and we have to be careful not to generalize about them ourselves.

ART: Some of them were very open and very nice, but some of the family didn't want us to be there. So for me it was a great opportunity to get better acquainted with the Hemings cousins. I think symbolically—for racial relations—we should be voted in. If they don't let us in, what kind of message is that sending to the rest of the country? They've got a lot of media attention now, and they could say, "We're moving forward and we're going to let you guys in. Whether the DNA evidence is positive or negative, we believe that you're family and we want to be a unit." Rather than [the association's] just being caretakers for the cemetery, the country could point to the association as a model in racial issues.

Shay Banks-Young is a matriarch of my family. She comes from a strong line running clear back to our common ancestor, Madison. I realize now, after getting together with Shay, that it has always been the women who have kept our family together. Shay is an activist in her community in Columbus, Ohio. She also has a strong spiritual foundation. Shay taught me a lot about our African roots, the true roots of the Hemings family tree.

Shay Banks-Young

MY MOTHER LIVED IN A HOUSEHOLD with her mother and her grandmother, and her great-grandmother came to visit. My mother's great-grandmother was a granddaughter to Thomas and Sally. Madison was her father. When you look at it from that perspective, it's not going back very far. When you think of it from that perspective, people say, "Well, you're talking about six generations!" My mother's great-grandmother was the first generation born out of slavery. They had just come from bondage. This is new to us. We have had just about a hundred and fifty years out of slavery. We spent four hundred years in, so we have had fewer years out of bondage than we had in. You just can't erase that and act like it didn't happen. That's why there are some black people who are so busy still being confused. We weren't allowed to be a family. You could love as long as you knew that that love was temporary. I give birth to you, my son, and even though you may come from the slave master, I still bond with you as my child. But they take you from me! I wasn't allowed to see my man lifted up and be anything of significance, so the black man is still struggling, trying to find his place, and society still puts him down. But somehow, through all of that, we still managed to survive. And the fact that we survived is the miracle. And not only survived! They gave us a legacy to behold, and we are a testament to them. We're their testament.

My contention is that blacks from Africa and blacks from America have a similarity because we brought our culture with us. And as much as they stripped us of everything, they couldn't strip us of our dignity and the soul of our spirit.

When I went to Senegal, Mali, Togo, Benin, Nigeria, Tanzania, Ethiopia, Zanzibar, and Egypt through a program with American Forum for International

Study in 1980, I was enlightened. One woman, who looked so much like me, said, "I knew my sister from America was back." And she said, "Is your father from America white?" I said, "Heavens, no!" And she said, "Well, how did you get to look like that?" I said, "Honey, it took us three hundred years to get like this. I didn't get like this overnight." They didn't realize what happened to us. In Nigeria, I met a man, the Obad, which is an honorary type of king, in his castle, or palace, and he apologized to us. "I want to apologize to you for selling you to the white man" is what he said to us. He said, "I want to apologize because it was a terrible thing for us to do. But your being sold has benefited us in many ways because of all the technologies and the things you've learned over the years, and now we need you to return home and bring the wisdom you have home to us again." I thought that was really interesting. We don't even realize the benefits of living in this country compared to those countries in Africa.

Unnamed African Woman—Captain John Hemings
Elizabeth Hemings—John Wayles
Sally Hemings—Thomas Jefferson
Madison Hemings

Harriet Butler Spears

Frances Butler Chapman

It all goes back to dealing with your roots—to go back and under-stand your heritage, and then pass it on. I'm a senior generation in my family. That's frightening for me. All our elders are gone. And it occurred to me that I have to be accountable for what I leave behind. I keep saying we need to learn to pass the banner down. I've been praying for someone to pop up in my family, somebody who would have an interest in my family who was younger. That's why I'm so happy that you're doing this book and passing on our history. Now our family story will never die.

I was lucky to meet Alex Haley back in the early seventies, when he was putting his book *Roots* together. He encouraged me. "You sit down and you talk to your elders in your family. You go get your old Bibles, get your birth certificates, your baptismal things, and you talk to these people, and you start keeping notes, collecting pictures, and constructing family trees. The interview process is also really strong and important."

A lot of people find it painful to trace back through their family heritage, because they feel it only goes back to slavery, and who wants to be a slave?

But our family tree goes way beyond slavery. It goes back to the continent of Africa, where our ancestors had their own culture, their own traditions, and their own religion. That is the heritage that is in our family, and that's what we must pass on.

| Ursel Chapman Hill | Frances Bernice Hill Harris | Sharon Shay Banks-Young | William Douglas Banks |

nlike my cousin Shay, who's always known who she is and where she comes from, Daniel Hemmings knows little about his family. He wonders if the reason he knows so little is because of a family secret—a possible black heritage. Dan and his wife, Mary, have worked hard to track his heritage back five generations to white coal miners in Virginia and Kentucky. But Dan's search continues. After being embraced by my family, Dan worries most that he may not, after all, be related. Regardless of where Dan's search leads him, he'll always be family to me.

Daniel & Mary Hemmings

DAN: I'm kin to every Hemings in Virginia. Everywhere we go, the first thing we do is open up the phone book to see if there are any Hemingses around. We've been kin to every Hemings in every phone book I've ever looked in. Now, we may be descended from some other Hemings at Monticello. There were lots of them, and not just from Sally, as you well know. There were lots of Hemingses, so although I think the possibility is great that we came from Monticello, we're not necessarily from Sally or Thomas! But we're Hemingses nonetheless.

I've seen Hemings spelled with one *m* and two. Sometimes it just depended on the way the census taker recorded it. On my birth certificate it's spelled with two.

MARY: Danny's father never told Danny anything about himself. Absolutely nothing.

DAN: Before my search I didn't know a thing about my grandfather, and I couldn't get any solid information from any of my family members, either. The only thing I knew was the way things seem to have been hush-hush all these years. But I had to try to find out something. That's pretty bad when you can't even trace back to your grandfather.

MARY: Because there's something about having family, a heritage, that teaches you to have a feeling of pride, to know who you are. If you don't know who your ancestors are, you don't have that feeling of belonging.

DAN: It wouldn't bother me to find out I was a descendant of the slaves up at Monticello. It wouldn't bother me the least little bit. I think it would be kind of neat. To me, it's a bigger deal to be a descendant of Sally Hemings than of Thomas Jefferson. That's the way I look at it. That's where all the courage came from: from the Hemings family. They're the ones who built that place.

MARY: And tore it down and built it up and tore it down on T.J.'s whim.

DAN: I don't know if it was serendipity or fate that we met Shannon and his family at the Monticello reunion back in May of '99, but there were so many little sequences that led up to that day. That morning we called Monticello hoping to start my genealogical search, and after I told them my name was Hemmings, they said, "Well, there is a family reunion going on and we would love to have you." The next thing we knew, we had on name tags and were up on that mountain.

MARY: That day at Monticello was a life-changing experience for Danny, and he's been different ever since. He said it was the strangest thing—even though he didn't know for sure if he was a member of the family and may never know—to be accepted with open arms like that.

DAN: I've never been accepted like that before, by total strangers. I felt like I could just relax, let my guard down. I felt totally at ease. I felt more comfortable with the family I met that day than I do with some of the family I've known my whole life.

When Mary and I went to the family dinner later that night at Michie Tavern, we got there late, so we sat down at a table with Jefferson descendants. When they saw my name tag, they looked down at me, not because of the probabilities of who I may be, but just the *possibility*. I couldn't believe it. I really felt a tinge of prejudice there, and it was a strange feeling for me. It was the same way I felt as a kid, when I had long hair and people followed me around in stores and thought I was going to take stuff. But as a grown man, it's the first time I had felt that—out of place, shunned, unwanted. It was strange.

Later, when I was telling one of my black friends at work about it, he said,

"Well, now you know a little bit of what I go through every time I wake up—
every day; just walking down the street. It's just a feeling that you carry with
you."

MARY: Shannon said he experienced some of the same kind of prejudice at
the meeting on Sunday. There was an elderly lady—about eighty or ninety years
old—and Shannon extended his hand to say, "Hi." He was all smiley, just wanting to meet some people after the meeting, and she didn't want to have anything
to do with him. She wouldn't even look him in the eye! She said, "Ugh! Get away

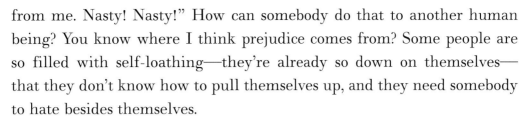

from me. Nasty! Nasty!" How can somebody do that to another human being? You know where I think prejudice comes from? Some people are so filled with self-loathing—they're already so down on themselves— that they don't know how to pull themselves up, and they need somebody to hate besides themselves.

DAN: Yeah, and for that lady to say that to Shannon, who was one of the most delightful people there! You know how Shannon is. He was probably saying, "Be blessed, have a nice day." But that lady seemed like she just didn't want any of that. No, no, no! Keep your blessings—and your niceness—away from me.

MARY: There was a man in a wheelchair that day. When his wife

introduced us as Hemingses, he just turned and wheeled away.

DAN: But there were also a lot of positive things that happened that the press never reported. There were Jeffersons who were very loving and open-armed, and then there were some who had never attended a Monticello Association meeting before, who chose to come to that meeting to embrace their new cousins.

MARY: I think that's what this story can do. That's the gift of it. It's a turning point in our history, in American history. The younger generation is looking for a way to heal this whole mess. They've grown up with each other— Latinos, blacks, whites, Russians, Chinese. They're all going to school together and they're friends, and they don't understand this division.

DAN: I had to overcome racism because I was brought up in a prejudiced environment. But after many years, with the help of my wife, I've shed that skin, and I've learned to take a whole different view: that people are people. This Hemings thing is history. The Jeffersons have to learn to live with it. You're not going to change history no matter what you do. But I'm proof that the cycle of racism can be broken.

MARY: Well, my father was from Alabama, the heart of Dixie, yet he was not a prejudiced person, nor was his family. He believed in treating everyone with respect, and that's the way he raised me. He was just a real decent man.

DAN: Together, Mary and I have raised two great sons. They don't think that they're better than anybody else or anybody else is better than them. I've broken the cycle of racism, and I'm going to get as many people as I can to break it as well. All we've got to do is help one or two people, and if they help one or two people, pretty soon we'll put an end to racism and the whole world will be healed.

Dan Hemmings leaves behind his racist past.

$\mathcal{L}$ike Dan, my great-uncle Frank Diggs, who we all call Teddy, has been doing some research into his own unanswered questions. Last year, at one of my family's camping trips, I sat in on a conversation with my uncle Teddy and his niece Brenda, my cousin. Brenda believes that she knows little more about Thomas Jefferson today than she did back in high school. There are also many things about our family that she doesn't know or was never told. These days, Brenda is a mother of three small children, and they seem to have millions of questions about where they come from. So Brenda hoped Uncle Teddy could help her find some of those answers.

Frank Diggs

TEDDY: I just came back from the Charlottesville area, where I went down to pick up some birth records. It's supposed to be where my dad's parents, Momma and Daddy Gaye, got married. My grandmother Momma Gaye, Martha Gaye Coles, has been dead over forty years and we still don't know much about her, because you didn't ask adults too many personal questions back then. That's why it's impossible to fully understand, because some things weren't talked about. What I do know is that Momma Gaye was Indian, or at least part, I think Blackfoot. That's what Daddy used to say, that's what he was told. But he's not sure if, back then, *they* even knew for sure.

To find out more, I recently went to the Getting Word exhibition at Monticello's Visitors' Center. It's got two pictures up of your dad, Jack, one of your first cousin, Billy Dalton, and all these other people all over the wall. And there was a woman there talking to me about the people on the wall who "think" they're descendants of Thomas Jefferson. She was at least nice about it, but she said we have no way of knowing for sure if they are descendants. And I wanted to say to her, "Well, if you can't tell where these black kids are from, how can you be so sure where the white ones come from? I'm whiter than you are, and I'm black." So to say that all those children that Jefferson supposedly had by his so-called wife were his may not be true, because he wasn't there a lot. You know, these plantations, they weren't thousands of acres all in one plot. They had property in Maryland,

Virginia, all over the place, and the owners would travel. And travel back then wasn't too fast. To travel a hundred miles took a long time. And you can't tell me that their wives were so pure that they might not have had a relationship with a slave back then. So how do you know that all those kids were his and not some white-looking slave's? If you honestly say that all the white kids were his, you'd have to say that the black kids were, too. It's fair.

I went to the courthouse in Charlottesville to look at birth records, and while down there, I ran into this woman who was a genealogist. She asked me for the names and dates I was looking for. She told me I wasn't going to find what I was looking for because there were no birth records or death records kept in Albemarle County for that period. They stopped keeping birth records and death records just after the Civil War, in about 1896, and they didn't start keeping them again until 1912. Now, you could go back *before* 1896 and find anyone you wanted, up until 1853. You know, most of the slave ships that came to Virginia came through the port cities like Jamestown and Williamsburg, and a lot of the slaves were sold off to towns like Charlottesville. That's why that missing period of time was critical.

People did have to record marriages back then. On the marriage certificate there was a place to indicate if you were colored or white. Most of the time the colored would have the mother's name listed and father as unknown. So it's really hard to know who's who. I guess it was a good way of getting around the whole thing. These days, we take the father's name. Back then it depended on the

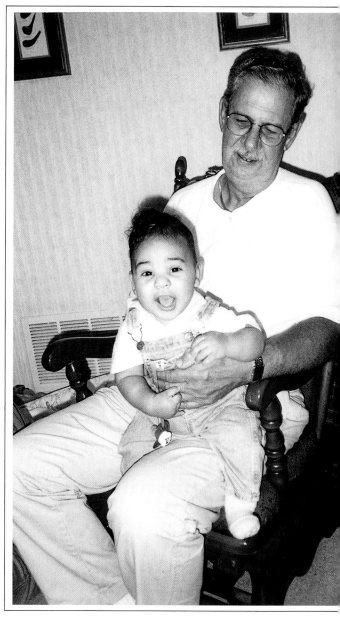

Uncle Teddy and grandson Simeon.

people's situation. They could have received their father's last name, or if their father were supposedly "unknown," they would receive their mom's last name. That's why it's very difficult to find things out.

Uncle Teddy and family around the campfire.

BRENDA: Why were there so many secrets? What kind of stuff do you think people were hiding? Was it parental stuff? Was it racial stuff? Was it who-raised-who stuff?

TEDDY: Well, when you go back to the days of, say, my great-grandparents, if a slave master wanted a slave woman, her husband couldn't say anything. If she got pregnant by the master and had a child by him, she and her husband would just raise the child as their own. That's just how it was back then. You didn't even think about it. There was nothing you could do about it, because they'd lynch you, they'd kill you, or you'd just disappear. So you kept your mouth shut.

BRENDA: What do you think your father and grandma were holding back or hiding from you?

TEDDY: Well, my dad's sister Aunt Carrie was not a full-blooded sister to him. She was a half sister. I'm not sure, but I was told that her father was the son of this man that Momma Gaye gave work to in their house. But Daddy Gaye and Momma Gaye never wanted to talk about that.

BRENDA: But that's what I don't get, why wouldn't they talk about it?

TEDDY: People just said, "Grand-momma told me, and she made me swear never to tell." So then you *don't* tell.

BRENDA: But what would they ever have to lose by telling?

TEDDY: At the time the promise was made, it could've been embarrassing for Grandmomma, you know, having children by different fathers. Aunt Carrie would be ninety-five to ninety-six years old now. You're talking about a situation that happened almost a hundred years ago.

BRENDA: My husband, Tom, knows nothing about his mom's side of the family. Tom's grandmother was born and raised in Czechoslovakia. His mother was adopted and came to the U.S. So consequently his mom really doesn't know anything. Unfortunately, that's true for many Americans.

TEDDY: It's hard not knowing anything. See, I know nothing of Momma Gaye's history. I remember when my wife, Charlene, and I went down to Diggs, Virginia—it's right on Chesapeake Bay. When we came to what we call a marina here, I went in and started talking to the guy there. I told him my name and that I was looking for some Diggs relatives so I could find out more about my family. So he said there's a lot of Diggses around here, just down the road. I went down there and this older gentleman started telling me things about the Diggses and so on and so forth. And I told him I appreciate all that you've been telling me, but I'm trying to find the *black* side of the Diggs family. And he said, "It don't make any difference. Y'all are related." He said, "We got white Diggses here, we've got black Diggses here, and they're all relatives. You know, it doesn't surprise us if you say you're black, 'cause we're not totally sure what *we* are." He said, "Just go to the cemetery down the road and take a look at the headstones."

I went down there and it was just full of Diggses, there was nothing but Diggses. I went back and told the man how surprised I was and he said, "Well, now you know, if your name is Diggs, y'all came from the same place. Same family."

*T*he descendants of Martha Jefferson have an easier time knowing who they are on paper. Jane Schluter is a descendant of Thomas Jefferson, through his daughter Martha Randolph, and wears the Randolph family ring, which has been passed down to her through the generations. Although there was a lot of tension at the Monticello Association meeting where we first met, it was not between Jane and me. We have since stayed in touch. I interviewed her at the beach near her home in New Jersey.

Jane Randolph Schluter

THERE'S ALWAYS BEEN THE LEGEND of Thomas and Sally's relationship. In my family, it was always referred to as a rumor propagated by the Hemings family. It was not until the Jefferson family reunion last year that I really had to consider it seriously. Despite my family's predetermined views, I wanted to hear the evidence and be able to make my own judgments.

I don't know the Hemingses' oral history and I'm not discounting it at all. But at the same time, suppose that Thomas Jefferson's brother raped or had an affair or relationship with Sally. It was probably better for Sally to say Thomas Jefferson was the father. I'm not trying to discount the oral tradition, but you also have to say that he was a public figure, very much in the public eye. Who would you rather have as a father for your kids, you know? It could happen. Couldn't it happen? I don't know. I wasn't there. Unfortunately, we don't have pictures or documents. I'd really like to know. It would be interesting. I know that it's coincidence that every oral tradition says the same thing, and I understand that there's a very good chance that it's true.

But I've always been told that Martha and Thomas Jefferson were so in love. They were famous for their great relationship. He loved her so much that I don't think he could ever have fooled around on her with Sally, but they say that after Martha died, it was a possibility. And they say Sally's the closest thing to Martha, being her half sister, but at the same time she's thirty years younger than Thomas. She could have even looked a little bit like Martha. Sally grew up in the household and she was obviously favored, too, because she was half sister to Martha and that's probably why she was a household slave.

We think it was his brother, if anyone. It could happen. I'm open to it. I don't know, I wasn't there. But at the same time with Thomas's reputation, I can't see him taking advantage of someone, and I think it would be taking advantage of the situation. That's why I have to rule Thomas out.

People may say Thomas fell in love with Sally after his wife died. Yes, it could have happened, but he's still thirty years older, and I do have a problem with the age difference. At the same time, he was a fascinating, very attractive man for his age, very accomplished. And you look at older men with those attributes and think, "Oh, wow! That's a very accomplished man. I really respect him." And you can be attracted to him because of the respect you have for him. I don't know, I wasn't there. There's no conclusive evidence.

You know what? We could go further back than Jefferson. We're all related because everybody intermarried. We were a noble family in Virginia, and everybody intermarried. I'm sure we're related to Lee, Madison, and Churchill, too. We're related to Churchill through Thomas Jefferson. Churchill's son was named Randolph—like my middle name—and his mother was American. I can trace my lineage very far back. For example, the famous figures Pocahontas and her husband, Captain John Rolfe, were at the very beginning. Back to England. I don't know how far beyond we can go, but it's traceable and well documented. So I can trace my line back pretty far and that's because I'm related to famous people.

My family history is well documented, and I definitely know who they are. But I've spent my entire life searching for a real sense of family, because I didn't have that growing up, although I do today. I never realized why I traveled so much, and it wasn't until I was "adopted" by a family in New Zealand that I realized that family was the most important thing to me. I would love to have more family. So, for me, it doesn't matter who you are or what race you are. When I met the Hemings descendants, I was impressed and taken by their warmth and immediate acceptance of me, even if I did not share the same opinion about Sally and Thomas. They accepted me without judgment and shared that same need to be part of a family that I had often felt. Now I can't wait to get to know them as family.

After talking with Jane, I started to wonder, "What is family?" Is family about common blood? Or is family a feeling of closeness based on common interests, on mutual respect and regard? My family has always been very close, but we never stop to think what that really means. It just *is*. My cousin Amanda and I grew up together. During a yearly family campout, Amanda, some cousins, and I stayed up all night talking about the family and the whole T.J. and Sally connection. Instead of concentrating on the DNA study, Amanda was much more interested in family and what it really means.

Amanda Pettiford

WE'RE A TRULY UNIQUE FAMILY. I don't think you could find a family with more racial diversity. But I could be related to anybody.

What if I found out that I was adopted? Do you think I would have any real attachment to my biological parents? No. My parents have been my parents for seventeen years! These other people would mean nothing to me. There's no relationship at all.

You could have someone come up to you on the street and say you're related, and there's no way to prove it. Like those people on the Martha Jefferson side. They didn't have to prove they were descendants of Thomas. How do you know they're not faking it? They may not even be in the family, but how would you know?

That's why I don't think you should feel obligated to love family just because they are family, especially if they haven't *been* family to you.

Look at all the kids who've been abused by their parents. I think that if somebody put me through all that, it would be real hard for me to love them. So how am I supposed to have emotions for these Monticello Association people I've never met? It's not that I hate these people. I don't have any emotions about them. I don't *know* them. I wouldn't even be hurt if they didn't accept me as a family member.

But I would be hurt if they didn't accept me as a person. You have to at least acknowledge my presence. If I come up to you and make the effort to talk to

Amanda with her cousin Meech.

you, you better talk back and respect me as a human being.

For example, after the *Oprah* show, I was talking with some friends and I told them that that was my family, and some of them didn't believe me. And one girl even called me a monkey! A monkey—because I'm mixed! I ate lunch with her all last year and I couldn't believe that she called me a monkey. I was ready to smack her upside her head! It really just made me laugh, because I look no different than her, and then she goes for a quick tanning before the prom and now *she* looks black!

Now, with my *real* friends, I love them to death. I love them just as much as I love my family and they're not related to me. There's no difference. Friendship and family need to go together. You have to be friends before you're family.

I think family means more than just blood. They can still step on your toes and disrespect you. They could disapprove of what you're saying. That doesn't make them any less of a family member.

Your family are the ones who are there for you during thick and thin, and you always hear, "I got your back and you got mine."

That's family.

L̲ucian K. Truscott IV is a fifth great-grandson of Thomas Jefferson, through his daughter Martha. He was raised to believe that all people are equal. Ten days after the DNA results were published, Lucian went on *The Oprah Winfrey Show* and extended a public invitation to his Hemings cousins to attend the Monticello Association family reunion. He said we should open our hearts and our arms and welcome our Hemings cousins into the family.

Lucian K. Truscott IV

MY BROTHER, FRANK, WAS ABOUT THREE and I was four and a half when, as fifth great-grandsons of Mr. Jefferson, we first laid flowers on his grave at Monticello in 1951. I have a clear memory of the weeks we spent in the early 1950s at Wild Acres, the last piece of land owned by our branch of the Randolph family in Virginia. We would play all morning in the creek behind the house. After a lunch of beaten biscuits and ham and fresh lemonade, we would be bathed and combed and dressed in shorts and white shirts and leather shoes and our great-aunts, Agnes and Miss Moo, would usher us in to see Gran, our great-grandmother Mary Walker Randolph.

Frank and I would stay for an hour in her bedroom, listening to her stories as she brushed her waist-length gray hair, handing us fistfuls so we could put it on her window ledge for the cardinals to build their nests with. Her grandfather was Thomas Jefferson Randolph. His grandfather was Thomas Jefferson. Thus, Mary Walker Randolph grew up with a man who had spent thirty-four years of his life with Mr. Jefferson. Between my ears and Mr. Jefferson's lips were only two people, one of whom was sitting in the room with us.

History has all the tension of a cheap Slinky and collapses as quickly when you think of how close we are to Mr. Jefferson, not in years but in human beings and what they have told us. My great-grandmother never told us that her grandfather had told her that Mr. Jefferson had had two families—one with his wife, Martha, from whom we descended, and one with his slave Sally Hemings. People didn't talk about miscegenation—not in Virginia back when it was still a crime they didn't. Most especially, they didn't accuse Mr. Jefferson of the crime of "race mixing." But there was another reason: Our great-grandmother was one of the founders of the Monticello Association, which has clung stubbornly to its oral history that someone—anyone—other than Mr. Jefferson fathered Sally's children.

But what of the oral history of Michele Cooley Quille or Phyllis Everett or any of

Lucian, his daughter, Lilly, and wife, Carolyn.

the other Sally Hemings descendants who, because I invited them, were accepted as guests by the Monticello Association at the family reunion for the first time in its eighty-six-year history? What of Shay Banks-Young, who told the *Washington Post:* "My mother's great-grandmother was Jefferson's granddaughter. It wasn't like we had to read a book or see a DNA test to know this." The stories they tell about who they are, and from whom they descended, were passed down from lips to ear, lips to ear, just as Gran passed along her stories to me and Frank.

I'll tell you what separates me and Frank from our Hemings cousins. The oral history of the Hemings descendants has not been accepted by historians because it was a history passed along by slaves. It is a history that has been denigrated and denied by the Monticello Association because many feel that if we come to accept that Mr. Jefferson had a family with Sally Hemings, this somehow damages his reputation.

Lucian K. Truscott, Jr., with his wife, Sarah Randolph Truscott, and their children, Lucian III, Mary, and James.

Lucian K. Truscott III and son Frank (above).

Anne Harloe Truscott and son Lucian (right).

It's hard for me to understand how you do further damage to the reputation of a man who owned slaves. It gave me hope to learn that she loved Tom enough that, for the last nine years of her life, after he died in 1826, Sally walked two or three times a week the six-plus miles up the mountain from her home in Charlottesville to the cemetery at Monticello to tend his grave.

It gives me hope that forty-seven years after Frank and I laid flowers on his grave, my daughter, Lilly, laid flowers on his grave not only with her cousins from Mr. Jefferson's family with Martha, but with her cousins from Mr. Jefferson's family with Sally. What does not give me hope is this: Sally Hemings is likely buried beneath what is now a Hampton Inn near Mr. Jefferson's beloved University of Virginia, and knowing this, the association continues to deny membership and burial rights to her descendants in the graveyard she tended so lovingly for so many years. This is an emotional issue for many of my white cousins because it involves the toxic Southern cocktail of land and blood and race. In denying rights to our black cousins, they have demanded documents as proof—birth certificates, even a letter from Mr. Jefferson himself acknowledging paternity. These pieces of paper do not exist: slaves were not permitted to write or to keep records of births, and Mr. Jefferson did not record the births of Sally's children as his because to have done so would have been to commit political and cultural suicide.

LUCIAN TRUSCOTT FAMILY TREE

Thomas Jefferson and
Martha Wayles Jefferson
↓
Martha Jefferson Randolph
↓
Thomas Jefferson Randolph
↓
Thomas Jefferson Randolph, Jr.
↓
Mary Walker Randolph
↓
Sarah Randolph Truscott
↓
Lucian K. Truscott III
↓
Lucian K. Truscott IV
↓
Lilly Truscott

Well, you cannot wish away the emotional entanglements of history any better than you can confirm them with papers and letters and official certificates, and this is how it should be, for a history devoid of emotion has no soul, and a history without soul is a history without meaning. So we'll be back, Frank and his family, and me and my family, and my sisters and their families. The first year we invited thirty-five of our Hemings cousins. The next year we'll bring a hundred, maybe more. We'll be back with our Hemings cousins at the association's annual reunion year after year after year until they relent. Hopefully, a day will come when this won't be a story about land and blood and race. One day it will be a story about an American family.

A few months after the reunion at Monticello, Lucian organized a small cookout at his home in Los Angeles. There I met Lucian's sister Susan and her daughter Rachel as well as Rachel's seven-year-old daughter, Sierra. Sierra is biracial and had been asking if there were other people in the family that were darker-skinned like her. Her uncle Lucian thought it would be a good idea to introduce her to some of her cousins who look like her—like me, for example!—as well as two Woodson elders, Jane Floyd and Edgar Love, who live in the Los Angeles area. We looked at photos and marveled at how much Lucian's grandmother looked like Jane Floyd.

Susan & Rachel Truscott

SUSAN: We have a very rich heritage from the Randolph side of our family. Everybody was very well educated. They thought that family was very important, as was integrity and how they carried themselves. They were true ladies and gentlemen. I was looking at Jane Floyd's photo album and reading the bios on all those people and it was the same family: all very educated, obviously very cultured, intelligent, and with a strong sense of family. The Hemingses even have a four-star general on their side, just like we have our uncle, a World War II hero. It was very, very exciting to see that.

RACHEL: I've heard some horror stories from friends who are in interracial relationships. People sometimes ask me, "Aren't you worried about your daughter Sierra, because she's biracial?" And I say, "Not in our family."

SUSAN: Unfortunately, not all of our Jefferson relatives are as open-minded. I think it's offensive what they're doing to the Hemingses. They never made us roll up our sleeves to give blood and prove we were related. Never.

Speaking of the graveyard, we were always told, "If you want to, that's where you can be buried." That was one of those things you grew up with. Now I don't know who will or who would want to. Of course, both of my parents are buried in the Monticello graveyard, and that kind of changes my feelings about it.

RACHEL: I really didn't know anyone there personally except Neanie, my grandma, and so it doesn't mean as much to me. And then it's so far away from us,

Three generations: Rachel, Sierra, and Susan.

too, since we live on the West Coast. I've always thought I'd want to be buried close to my family, and if it ends up that that's where all my immediate relatives decide that they're going to be, then that might be something I would consider.

SUSAN: Well, I grew up as a military brat, so to me that seems perfectly natural. Everybody always lives in different places, so why shouldn't they be buried really far away? I went to a different school every year of my life. We spent time in Germany. My dad was stationed in Japan; that's where Lucian was born. We went to Hawaii twice and many other places in the United States. It seemed like we were always moving.

Jane Floyd with Carolyn, Susan, and Rachel Truscott.

Well, unbeknownst to us kids, my mother was saving a lot of things—like all of the letters any of us ever wrote her, and cards, everything. It's not like my parents lived in the same house for fifty years. They moved thirty-one times and had to take all this stuff with them. And I'm really glad they did.

Now that my father has passed away, my brothers and sisters and my daughter Rachel and I have all come together to go through their belongings. It's been quite a walk down memory lane. We found a lot of photographs. The really old ones are mounted on black paper with the little triangle things on the edges. They wrote on the paper under the

*Jane Floyd holding
a photo of herself.
Note her resemblance
to Susan and Lucian
Truscott's grandmother,
Sarah Randolph
Truscott* (inset).

photos with either white or silver ink. And then we found diaries from my grandmother, which were very interesting. We've even come across letters that my dad wrote to Mother when he was in Korea.

RACHEL: We also found what Poppie, my grandpa, called *The Jefferson Connection*. It is our family tree, which he drafted in 1978, and it's really detailed. It has all the dates, births, deaths, marriages, all the children, and it shows exactly how we're all related. It's interesting to look at the dates and how young people were when they died and how a lot of parents named their children after a child that had died. On the back of *The Jefferson Connection*, Poppie wrote: "If you're like me, you probably often wondered, 'Just how am I related to Jefferson, the Eppes, the Taylors, and the Ruffins?'"

SUSAN: One of the things I found in my dad's stuff was a paper he wrote when he was a military cadet at West Point in 1943. I'll read you the last paragraph. "Perhaps as important as the question of what honor is is the one asking, 'Are all men born with honor?' We all wonder this at one time or another. We all wonder if God truly created all men equal. Did God endow the little colored shoeshine boy on the corner with as much or more or less than he gave me? Was I bequeathed as high a sense of honor as were Washington and Jefferson and Lincoln? I believe I was. I most ingenuously believe that all men were born equal as far as honor is concerned, and not only that, I believe that the spark remains alive and vibrant throughout our lives."

I have to think if my dad was saying that at the age of twenty-two—and to have been raised by parents who called black people "darkies"—he broke the mold. He became much more enlightened and, therefore, raised us that way. I think my dad and my mother were sort of enlightened before their time. The military had desegregation much earlier than the civilian world, and my dad was always its champion. He was all for equal rights. He was very open-minded and freethinking, and that's the way we were raised.

My dad taught me about honor and integrity. Now I see things in a different light. Going through the things my parents saved, I realized how much they've taught us. Now I'm thinking, "Maybe I won't toss this or that. Maybe I'll keep this." I'm not just thinking for me anymore; I'm thinking for my three girls and their kids. I want to pass on my family's legacies, because the people who came before you give you a sense of who you are.

Family is now, family is in the future, and family is in the past—the recent

The Truscott family after paying respects at the Monticello gravesite.

and the distant past. People should talk to each other and share their stories now. Don't wait until it's too late. You don't have to be related to Thomas Jefferson to find fascinating stories about your family. Go to your parents, go to your grandparents. And if you're lucky enough to have great-grandparents, go to them. Have them identify pictures and tell you stories, because someday it's going to mean a whole lot to you.

At Lucian's cookout, I had the opportunity to meet two of the family's elders, one of whom is Mrs. Jane Floyd. Mrs. Floyd is in her eighties. She is a retired schoolteacher who continues to educate everyone she meets. She has always believed in equality in education. In 1947, she spearheaded a movement that resulted in the integration of the Catholic schools of St. Louis. During the time we spent together in Los Angeles, she helped me understand how important and valuable our elders really are.

Jane Floyd

THE LEGACY OF SALLY HEMINGS AND THOMAS JEFFERSON is just an example of what happened in the South in the days of slavery. There were many mixed-race children born during those days, and every black family can trace their history back to one of them. That's the reason there are so many varieties of colors of black people. They didn't get that way by accident. So, we are an amalgamated group, mixed with many other races. You can hardly find a true black African anymore, even in Africa. They're of different skin hues, too; they're not black. Black is just a word anyway. Nobody's really black. Nobody's really white. I have said all along that we will never be at peace until everybody is mixed up. When we're all mixed up, maybe we'll get along.

That's what I say to the young people, but at the same time, be proud of your heritage. I would never pass over into the white race, which I and all my family could have done. One member of my father's family passed for white, but I was too proud. I will always be proud to be black because black people have so many virtues—perseverance, integrity, a keen sense of humor—by reason of having overcome mistreatment. There isn't a black person in this world who hasn't faced discrimination and prejudice. I don't think there's one, not one, whether they pass for white or not. They have developed a stamina that you don't find in others, except those who have similarly suffered. We have been forced into the fire, so to speak, and we have become a better people.

Your generation might think that racism doesn't exist anymore, but don't

A reunion of Jeffersons and Hemingses in Los Angeles.

kid yourself, it's still around. Once, when I was applying for a job as a school principal, I was told that I was too fair-skinned. If they were going to hire a black person, they wanted that person to be noticeably black, so that they could get credit for it. That is discrimination, and I've been very bitter about it. Very bitter. I'm sorry that I have to expose you to it, but that's what happens after eighty-seven years. Oh, I'm not saying we haven't made gains. We have. The situation in this country has been dramatically improved, but there's still so far to go.

Now the new generation will build bonds with the people they work with, but we didn't have that luxury. Years ago, we had to depend on our circle of friends from city to city to city. When we traveled, we had to depend on each other to sleep and eat. That developed a whole system of kindred spirits. Blacks knew blacks all over the country. We knew all of the black celebrities because we all faced the same discrimination. It's a chain that is difficult to understand if you haven't been used to it. If you want to know more, read the history of the NAACP. That's the biography Roy Wilkins wrote just before he died.

Young people don't seem to realize how powerful segregation and discrimination were. Our advances didn't come from just marching in the streets. Marching in the streets lent a lot of weight to the pleas to change the system, but you could march in the streets for a century and get nowhere if there's nobody on the inside working for you. The NAACP had Clarence Mitchell lobbying everyone in Congress. The NAACP played a big role in opening up opportunities for blacks. People these days think that there was nothing done about civil rights before Dr. Martin Luther King, but the fight for our rights started with the first runaway slave. People should look as far back as Frederick Douglass, who was a former slave, and many others who were very important to the civil rights struggle.

I came up in black schools in St. Louis. Every morning in high school we had an assembly in the auditorium and sang "Lift Every Voice and Sing," which James Weldon Johnson wrote for the NAACP. We'd spend an hour in the auditorium learning about black history. But who's to teach it now? Nobody's really qualified to teach it anymore. The problem is they've changed it so much. These days, black history only starts with the struggles in the sixties and Dr. King's March on Washington. Most people don't even realize how many contributed to that march, such as A. Philip Randolph of the Brotherhood of Sleeping Car Porters, Walter Reuther of the AFL-CIO, and Roy Wilkins of the NAACP.

These days, I cut out every piece of information I get from magazines and books and give them to my granddaughter so she'll know a little something. She has come up through the white schools in upstate New York and she doesn't know a thing about black history, so I'm trying to educate her. Roy Wilkins and I talked about this years ago. I said, "Now, who's qualified to teach black history?" Every old person knows black history, but they're not the ones in the schools teaching it. Now it's all word of mouth, like the legacy of Thomas Jefferson and Sally Hemings.

Although my mother was named Jane after Jefferson's mother, and of course I was named after my mother, I didn't learn about my fifth-generation direct ancestor, Thomas and Sally's firstborn, Thomas Woodson, until I was grown. My mother told me the big, dark secret right before I was married, and she said, "Don't tell anybody," because it was disgraceful to be illegitimate. When she was getting married, if her fiancé's family had known of her lineage, they might not have considered her worthy. So my mother kept it a secret, and so did I. I didn't even tell my sister until the Woodson Association sent me a letter about the first family reunion in 1976. I didn't go that year, but when I finally did, I felt right at home, and when I heard all the history of the families there, it tied right in with my mother's history. I felt like I really belonged with them, and I enjoyed going to the reunions very much.

I inherit a lot from my mother and her family, including my occupation. My mother was a teacher, my sister was a teacher, my aunt was a teacher, and my three great-aunts were teachers. Back in my day you became either a teacher or a nurse, because those were the only opportunities that were open to black women. Finally, I seized the opportunity to be a social worker when that opened up because of the Depression. I graduated from teachers college, but it was during the Depression, in 1933, and there weren't any openings for teachers, but there were plenty of openings for social workers, so I worked for the St. Louis Relief Administration for nine years. Finally, I was able to get a job in teaching. My whole teaching experience, except for four years of my twenty-seven years in education, was as a master teacher, teaching other teachers.

I worked with the League of Allied Arts Corporation, which is a group of fifty black women that devote themselves to promoting art in the black community. I was president of that organization for two terms. The average white person thinks there is no black art, but there's a whole wealth of it. People just don't know about it. Like the famous painter Henri Kaiser, who, incidentally, is a cousin of my husband.

I remember when the League of Allied Arts put on an exhibit some years back of an extensive drum collection from all over the world. The Smithsonian is showing the same exhibit. Now, that is recognition of black culture.

Well, I could go on and on for days. There's so much to be proud of and a whole lot more to learn. Unfortunately, you don't really learn until you get old. I guess old age does have some advantages.

At the cookout, I had the pleasure of meeting another of the Woodson family elders, Edgar Love. After working for the military overseas, he received his doctorate in political science from the University of Southern California. He went on to teach political science until his retirement in 1985. Edgar Love has overcome many hardships in his life but remains a strong and positive gentleman.

Edgar Forrest Love

My name is Edgar Forrest Love. I was born in 1919. That makes me eighty-one years old. I am a fifth-generation descendant of Thomas Woodson. I didn't find out about my ancestry until some twenty years ago, when I started tracing my roots.

I have considerable reservations about Thomas Jefferson. There's a hypocrisy about him that irritates me. Yes, he wrote the Declaration of Independence, but he was also a slave owner. Not a little slave owner, either. He had many slaves who served him. Now, how do you square with this? One question I ask myself, you hear people talking about "good slave owners." Can you be a *good* slave owner? I'm more proud of what my relatives on the Hemings side accomplished than the accomplishments of Thomas Jefferson, who had all the advantages. He came from rich parents and had a fine education, whereas our ancestors came from scratch, so to speak.

Today we are still suffering from the impact of slavery in the United States. I was born in what I describe as a "pigmentocratic society." Color determined everything in Missouri—where I'd go to school, who I could marry, and whatnot. At school we had to recite the Pledge of Allegiance. The Pledge talks about "justice for all." I remember one day—I must've been in the fourth grade then—as I was giving the Pledge, I looked across from me and saw one of my friends, a boy who came from a town about seventy-five miles from Kansas City. His brother had been lynched. They hung the body from a flagpole outside the school! People from Kansas City even drove up to see the lynching. Now, that's hatred with a passion. I wondered how my classmate felt. I wondered how he reacted to this idea of "liberty and justice for all." This was in the 1920s. In the

1920s, in most places, blacks couldn't tie a knot, let alone vote. So, yes, Thomas Jefferson did a lot of things as President, but he was also a slave owner. And in my book, slavery was bad. It was cruel. It was evil and immoral, and yet lasted for more than two centuries in our country.

When you stop and think about it, slavery wasn't that long ago. My grandmother, on my father's side, was born a slave. Of course, she didn't tell me this. Nobody in the family discussed it. My grandmother couldn't read or write, so I'd read the newspaper to her. I was a young boy. I didn't understand why she'd ask me to read to her. In those days, people just didn't talk about slavery. I guess she was ashamed of the fact that she'd been born a slave.

One way out of slavery was education. On my mother's side of the family, the Woodson side, there has always been a tremendous interest in education, all the way back to Thomas Woodson. He was a remarkable individual. He was forward-thinking. He sent his daughter Sarah Jane Woodson to Oberlin College, where she received her degree in 1856. This was something for a woman back then, especially a black woman. She then went on to teach at Wilberforce University. The Woodsons were not only well educated, but were educators themselves, and even helped found several learning institutions.

My father died when I was only three years old, and my mother proceeded to make our house a boardinghouse. She had teachers there. When I was nine, my mother died, and I went to live with my aunt, who was also a teacher. So I guess I was always surrounded by teachers, and I sort of assumed that I was going to be a teacher, especially since education helped set my spirit free.

But my spirit wasn't always free. I'll give you an example. Around 1935, I got on the train in Kansas City. I was headed to Oklahoma City, to visit my brother. It was a nice train—streamlined, air-conditioned—but before we entered the South, a black porter came around, got all the black people up out of their nice, comfortable seats, and moved them to the dilapidated Jim Crow car, which was on the front part of the train. I can remember looking at all those white people as I walked to the Jim Crow section. We'd paid the same amount of money, but here *we* had to get up.

It's kind of hard to describe how that felt. But I had a friend that could relate. He'd been put in a concentration camp in Austria. He once told me about an incident involving his father in Vienna. When the Nazis took over, all the Jews had to wear the yellow Star of David. For some reason, my friend's father had to go to a town outside of Vienna. He was very fearful, very reluctant to go. When he got on the train, he had to have on his Star of David. He must have felt like I did—conspicuous, and surrounded by people who hated him.

You never really knew what was going to happen. In 1958, I was working for a special project at the University of Southern California called the Pakistan Project. We brought over officials from Pakistan for special training. My job was to be the intermediary between the Pakistanis and the administration; for that I was made an honorary Pakistani. We made a tour of the United States, including the South. When we were on our way to El Paso, Texas, we stopped at this small-town restaurant.

Some of the Pakistanis were dark-complexioned, and people started looking at us. A big Texan punched me on the shoulder and said, "You boys colored?" I said, "We are Pakistanis. We are traveling. There is our car from the University of Southern California, and we're on our way to El Paso." So he told them to serve us, and they did. Looking back, I must have been crazy! Stopping in a small town in Texas!

We had another incident; this was in Knoxville, Tennessee. We went into a cafeteria at twelve o'clock, when it was full. The people at the counter didn't know what to do. Then one of the managers came up to one of my friends, a white fellow, and said, "We don't serve colored here." My friend said, "These are

Pakistani officials. We're visitors!" The manager threw up his hands, and we were allowed to eat there. When we were getting ready to go, the manager came over and said, "I hear that you're leaving early in the morning, so we're going to set up this room here so that you can get up and eat right away." Hiding us from the customers. I'll never forget those incidents in 1958.

The uncertainty was always there. You just knew that you had to be careful. If you crossed the line, something was going to happen, but sometimes you didn't know where the line was. It made it tough when you were traveling. Most blacks when they were traveling across the country, driving, would stop in towns where they knew someone. Or someone would tell them, "When you get to Little Rock, go to such-and-such a place. There you won't have any problems." I remember when Joe Louis had a fight in Kansas City, and he couldn't stay at any of the white downtown hotels, and there were just a couple of dilapidated black hotels. So Joe Louis rented my uncle's house. Joe Louis stayed at my uncle's house while he was training for the fight!

Even as a young boy I remember problems. Every summer I used to go to a boys' camp run by the Rotary Club. Now, black Boy Scouts could not go to the Boy Scout camp, which was near Kansas City. So the Rotary Club would let us go to their camp on the last week the camp was in session. Why do you think we went the last week? Here was the reason. There was a swimming pool, and after we left, they could empty the pool.

I came up in a black AME church. Once a year we used to have what was called Brotherhood Sunday. You couldn't guess what happened on Brotherhood Sunday. On Brotherhood Sunday, our pastor would take his choir, go over to a white church, and preach. The white pastor would come to our church. That was Brotherhood Sunday. I used to look at the windows of our church, and they had all kinds of pictures of angels on them. The angels were white. Here I am going to a black church with white angels. I don't know whether I concluded that there were no black angels or we didn't get into heaven or not, but it was humiliating, it was degrading—it engendered self-hate. I remember a saying. How does it go? "If you're black, get back. If you're brown, stick around. If you're white, you're all right."

Luckily, there were some people who tried to instill pride in being black. Yeah, I know we should be over this race thing already, but we aren't and it's been two thousand years.

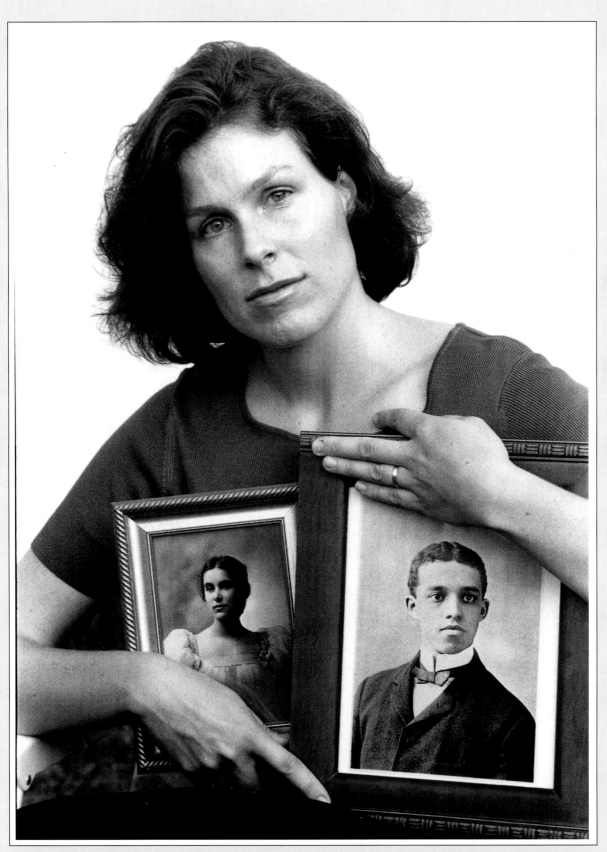

Jill Sim embraces photos of her great-grandmother and great-uncle,
among the first African-American graduates of, respectively, Vassar College and MIT.

dgar Love and Jill Sim have been communicating by e-mail for years. Jill describes herself as feeling rootless her whole life, as if she didn't fit into any one group. She always classified herself as "other." Jill had a close relationship with her grandmother Ellen but always felt as if there was something missing. Soon after her grandmother's death in 1994, bits and pieces of the puzzle began to fall together, and the family secret was revealed to her. I flew from California to Virginia to talk to her about it.

Jill Sim

MY GREAT-GRANDMOTHER ANITA HEMINGS was the first African-American graduate of Vassar College, in 1897. This was my family's well-kept secret. Grandma's mother had been born [a light-skinned] black, and she had left her black family behind to become white, an irreversible decision—a decision that would affect all the future generations of the family. I thought of my faceless black ancestors who watched their daughter Anita leave them behind for better opportunities, for a better life, as a white woman. She had to pass as white to educate herself. She had to abandon the very core of who she was to educate herself. My great-grandmother was the first black graduate of Vassar, and if the family had had its way, I never would have known about it.

By all accounts, Anita was an impressive student who had mastered Latin, ancient Greek, and French and, as a soprano in the college choir, had been invited to sing solo recitals at the local churches in Poughkeepsie. She was also known around the college for her "exotic" beauty. Many of her classmates tried to guess at Anita's origins; some thought she might be of Native American descent. According to the *New York World*, "Yale and Harvard men [were] among those who sought favor with the brunette beauty."

This fact may have fomented some jealousy in Anita's roommate, who had begun to have suspicions regarding Anita's racial identity. I learned that shortly before Anita was set to graduate, the roommate persuaded her own father to investigate the Hemingses. He traveled to Boston to look up Anita's family. He found what he was looking for. The father of Anita's roommate returned to Vassar

College to drop a bomb: The beautiful and tawny fellow student Anita Hemings was indeed a Negress.

Her fellow students felt betrayed and embittered by Anita's deceit, and a school board went into special session to decide if Miss Hemings should be allowed to graduate after perpetrating such a falsehood. But Anita did graduate, and that summer the news of a black woman at white Vassar echoed through major cities in the United States and to "all corners of the globe," according to one paper covering the scandal. And today Anita is a great source of pride for Vassar.

I have an overwhelming feeling of pride for my great-grandmother, for the courage and strength she had shown in her quest for education. How alone she must have felt at the moment, almost exactly a century ago, when the news hit the college. I could only imagine the resources she had to draw on to weather the scandal and the subsequent affront felt by the Vassar community.

What white students and faculty might have seen merely as an insolent charade was in reality an agonizing and split existence. All through her college years, Anita shuttled back and forth between elite white Vassar and migrant black Boston, between rich white strangers and her poor black family.

A natural question after learning about all this was: What was that family like? Anita must have had extraordinary parents, who would have encouraged her to pursue her dream of becoming "thoroughly educated" (as she put it on one school application) as the sole black among many whites. Anita's parents and siblings would have agonized along with her; been afraid for Anita, for all four years when she was passing as white.

Later I was also told there was a brother of whom Anita was very proud. Frederick John Hemings graduated in 1897 from MIT, and MIT sent me what they could about him. He was listed as "Colored" in the school records and was one of MIT's first black graduates. I read that he went on to work all his life at the Boston Navy Yard as a chemist. Frederick, unlike his sister, never passed for white. Gazing on the copy of his school photograph, I saw a man whose physical features were much like my older brother's, but decidedly darker. I was looking at the first image of my black family.

When I was shown a picture of a young Anita Hemings for the first time, I fell in love with my great-grandmother's picture. Seeing the young Anita was like finding another missing link, the spine of the skeleton.

Harrison, Jill, and Alan Sim.

Over one hundred years ago, my great-grandmother Anita Hemings was exposed before Vassar College. Yet she stayed the course. And she did another brave thing. She sent her daughter, my grandmother Ellen, to Vassar. My grandmother successfully passed as white at Vassar, graduating exactly thirty years after her mother. By 1927, my family had faded to white.

Shawn, Priscilla, and Shannon Lanier.

While Jill has had to piece together her family's history, mine has always been with me thanks to my mom, Priscilla. She's the one who shared my family's oral history with me and my older brother, Shawn. My mother has always raised us to be proud of who we are. She herself is very light-skinned, so she was glad that my father had a darker complexion. That way her children would always know that they were black and be proud of it. With a master's degree in education, she has been teaching special education with multi-handicapped students for twenty-five years. She was my very first teacher.

Priscilla Lanier

I TEACH JUNIOR HIGH SCHOOL, and I've told different people at school that I'm a descendant of Sally Hemings and Thomas Jefferson. When my school was going to have a black history program last year, I wanted to present my lineage. I had already presented it to my class. But the principal didn't want me to. She said it was too controversial. Do you know what that principal asked me? She said, "What do you go by, black or white?" I said, "Well, according to society, if someone has one drop or one-tenth of black blood, then they're black. So I'm black." And she said, "But you don't look black. You could go any way you want." And I told her, "But I am black and I'm proud of my heritage." This year, she asked me to participate in the program. So as you can see, times are changing.

I want people to realize that black people come in all different shades and complexions. They can have all different textures of hair and even different-color eyes. Sometimes Shannon had problems when he was younger. The schoolkids would say, "Your mama is white." I told him, "Take in my birth certificate and point out the word 'Negro'; that'll show them that I'm not white." We always found it upsetting to have to prove who we were.

Now, there were people in my family that had two birth certificates, one that said they were black and one that said they were white. Because some chose to be white, there are people out there who have the same blood I have, but we don't even know each other. That's why I think it's important for people to know their family history and to come together as a family. There are so many people who are divided. That's what has happened all through the years. There were so many secrets, and nobody let it all out.

At one time, my mother and father sort of passed for white. This was when Daddy worked at a country club in Illinois. He said, "No one asked us if we were black, so we didn't tell them." But Daddy realized that if they stayed there, they couldn't ever have family visit who were darker-skinned. They decided they could not live like that for the rest of their lives—to be separated from their loved ones; hiding and worrying about what people thought, or might do—so, soon after, they moved back to Chillicothe.

I can also remember when my boys were young and we were living in rural Georgia, four hours south of Atlanta. I went for a job interview, and the principal said, "How do you feel about teaching black children?" I said, "All children have to be educated no matter what their race, no matter what their handicap. I've taught all kinds of students." Well, I got the job, and on the first day of classes I went into the school with Shawn and Shannon. I said, "I'm ready to enroll my two sons." And they said, "Well, where are they?" I thought, *"Oh, my God! They think I'm white!"* When he realized I was black, that principal gave me a heck of a time. He even told me that I would not be back next year. He said, "You're a darn good teacher, darn good teacher, but you won't be back. And you know the reason why." I always felt so inferior when I lived in Georgia. I didn't even take my kids to the store with me, because I was so scared for their lives. People would look at us like, "What's this white woman doing with these black kids?" Racism was rampant there. Here in Ohio, it's kind of swept under the rug. You may know someone hates you because of your color, but they don't come out and tell you.

The second and final year we lived in Georgia, I taught at a different school, and one parent came into my class and said, "I'm so glad Tommy has you for a teacher! Because he's done had them nigger teachers and they ain't taught him nothin'." At the end of the year, I couldn't get a babysitter and had to go to a parent conference with Shawn and Shannon, and that same parent looked at me with complete disgust. I remember another time, before I was married, a parent and child came up to me, and the child said, "Miss Dalton, there's your boyfriend!" Gerald—who was then my fiancé—was volunteering that day, and the parent said, "You're marrying a black man? What do your parents think about this?" I said, "They don't have a problem with it because I'm black, too." The

parent didn't speak to me for the rest of the year. My supervisor called me over and said, "Priscilla, it's kind of hard when we're trying to teach the kids the difference between black and white and then there comes you." I said, "I can't help that. That's the way it is." My race does not determine whether I'm a good teacher. I *am* a good teacher. I care about my kids and the way they learn, and so it shouldn't matter whether I'm black, white, or whatever.

You aren't born racist. You have to be taught. I teach handicapped children. They don't see color. They don't see you as black or white. No kid has ever called me a name in all the years I've been teaching. I've got white kids and black kids, and we're just one big happy family in the classroom, and maybe that's the lesson my students—and my family—can teach us all!

illy Dalton is my mom's youngest brother and also has a fair complexion. To me, he's always been like an older brother. He encourages me to do my best, to remember where I come from and how important family is. Uncle Billy is also the one who made sure I experienced the Monticello Association meeting by driving me down there with my cousins Troy and Vincent.

William Dalton

IMAGINE COMING UP LOOKING LIKE ME. I came up in a black neighborhood looking like a little white boy, with straight hair and everything. I never felt black enough. Everybody made fun of my hair, so I put vinegar in it. I messed it up. I tried to put curlers in it to get an Afro. Everyone else could grow Afros. Everybody had big 'fros, man! I didn't have that kind of hair, and I hated it.

I wasn't accepted by the black community or the white. I was this oddball. People always wanted to talk to me about race. I'd get asked, "What are you?" I'd tell them I was black, and sometimes they wouldn't even believe me. In college, it got to the point where I was so sick of people worrying about my color that I got a chip on my shoulder. If someone asked me anything about it when I'd first meet them, I'd think, "Oh! Color matters to you? Well, you're out."

I've never denied my blackness. I'm black. My sister, Priscilla—who's ten years older than me—told me a story about when I was only like three years old. I walked into the all-white country club where my dad worked, singing, "Say it loud! I'm black and I'm proud." Here's this little white boy singing the James Brown song he'd heard his older brother and sister singing and dancing to. This was back in the sixties, before Dr. King was shot. I can imagine me doing that because I went through a serious identity crisis. I'm still going through it! Not only did I have to come to grips with my blackness, but I'd look in the mirror every day and wonder where my whiteness came from. Now I know how far back it goes—clear back to Thomas Jefferson. And since I know how deep-rooted it is, I'm having an identity crisis with the white in me! You deal with this down to the core of your self. The whole deep thought of who I am, where do I come from, and do I come from "better stock," as my father used to tell me when he was disciplining me as a kid. Now I know what stock I come from.

I was born two days after Kennedy was shot. I came up through the struggle, through the seventies. I watched the Chicago riots and the war on TV. I was part of what was happening to this country. When my friends in school were saying, "Man, these people are nuts! We gotta do something about this," I'd say, "Well, let's get active and make some changes."

When we were at Monticello in '99, it was easy to understand what it might have been like to live on that hill, no matter what color you were. Unfortunately, the media had to turn it into a circus. "Let's stir it up!" That's what the media loves to do, and in the process it helped to create a very combative environment. But that's not good for America. That's not healing America! I went down there to heal America! I went down there to show my face, to show these people, "Look at me. You know who I am. I'm here to put my hand out to you. Don't act like this. Let's be friends. And, yes, America's watching us right now."

There were, of course, some people on both the Jefferson and Hemings sides who wanted to fight. But that ain't cool. That ain't what's good for America. That just keeps racism going. Here we are, the young people of America coming up—the descendants of this great man—and *we're* going to keep racism going? That isn't what he would've wanted. So that's why I'm probably not going back next year. I don't want to be part of all that Hatfield and McCoy–type feuding.

I want peaceful resolution. I want to have harmony amongst my extended family. We are the oldest and probably one of the largest known families in America, with the ability to trace our lineage back to our original ancestors. That's huge! I believe the godlike thing to do is to make a progressive stance and take an active part in the future of this nation. Our friends and families are America. And that's what it's all about: finding family, joining family, and being family.

My goal has always been to make a difference on this big ol' planet! One way would be to find the slaves' cemetery at Monticello and put up a monument. My brother Diggsie is a businessman, and we've come up with the idea of having the family chip in a chunk of money to a monument pot. Then we ask Monticello to match our chunk, and then we go together to the federal government and say, "Match our chunk." I know Monticello is already making efforts to do some restoration, but maybe we can help get it done faster.

Maybe in time we will all look at ourselves differently. These days, when I look in the mirror, I don't see black or white, I see A-M-E-R-I-C-A. I see America, and what America is. This is the face of AMERICA.

ike my uncle Billy, my cousin Nina sees herself first as an American. It was a dream of Nina's to meet more of her family, and her husband, Rusty, made that possible for her when he took her and their two small children, Lucy and Madison, to the 1999 Monticello reunion where we first met. While she was there, she nursed her newborn son, Madison, and wondered how Sally must have felt when she stood on that same land and nursed her own Madison. Though this was a very personal experience for Nina, she was bombarded by the press. Nevertheless, as a family diplomat, she conducted herself with the same quiet dignity that she believed her grandmother Momma Lucy would have exhibited. For Nina it all boils down to family—a family that, in time, without the media circus, will, she hopes, come to know and embrace one another.

Nina Balthazar-Boettcher

MY PARENTS NEVER ADDRESSED THE QUESTION OF RACE. Never. What am I? I'm a child of God. Until I was twelve or thirteen, we lived primarily overseas. We were Americans, and that was all there was to it. When we were in the Philippines, I do remember seeing the L.A. race riots on television, and it scared me to death. I couldn't understand how anybody could terrorize someone else, demean them just because of their color. That terrified me, and I was so grateful that I wasn't in America. That's one of the things I liked best about traveling. You didn't break down into little subcategories like everybody does now. We were all Americans!

My mother didn't raise me as a black woman. If you're not raised as a black woman, you don't just wake up one day and say, "Today I'm going to be a black woman." You have to learn how. I think it's a lot of work. A lot more is put on you, more so today than at any other time, because there

Lucy, Rusty, Nina, and baby Madison.

are so many people who are looking at you to do the right thing and say the right thing. It's hard. But I wasn't really raised white, either. So I can't wake up and say, "Well, I'd better get busy being white and start watching Sandra Dee."

So I've been on the fence my whole life. I honestly thought that "American" was a nationality. And when my mom taught me, she said, "Nationality means to what nation you swear your allegiance." When people kept pushing me about my background, she told me to ask them, "Does it matter?"

I tell people that I'm multiracial, and I tell my children they're blended. "Blended" sounds so much nicer than "mixed." "Mixed" sounds like something that happens to dogs, or something I do in the kitchen with flour and an egg. It doesn't sound like what happens when two people fall in love and get together. It's intentional. It's something that was created special, like if you have a fragrance that's blended especially for you. Well, my children are blended. They're special. And my son is named Madison, so he's not going to have to wonder if he's part black. He's going to know he was named for the patriarch of my family, a black man whose name was Madison Hemings. My children, Madison and Lucy, are going to know that their ancestors made a really big difference in the way people live in the world today, and that they had a lot to do with the founding of America. That's important.

Somebody once called the Hemingses the First Family of Slavery.

I thought about it, and that is unfair to other families that experienced slavery. The Hemingses were enslaved for about three generations and then freed. Because they were held in high regard, they ran Monticello. They never knew the great physical discomfort that usually goes hand in hand with slavery. I don't think they did much of the bump-and-grind, sweat-of-your-brow, and hauling-bricks stuff at Monticello and the University of Virginia. They had more to do with the design and conception, the architectural ideas. They were the masons. They ran the nail factory. They were building the colleges, and their kids were put into jobs where they learned trades. A lot of people don't think that a slave or a black man could have envisioned something as grand as Monticello or U.Va. and actually carry it out. But my ancestors did.

Do I think it was love between Sally and Jefferson? What speaks to me most is that Sally stayed in Charlottesville until she died so she could take care of that man's grave. Now, you know that if a man held you in bondage against your will, as soon as he was fertilizer you'd pack up and move. Wouldn't you? But instead, she tries to plant posies on Jefferson's grave. Our lineage in Ohio doesn't even start until she died because her boys wouldn't leave their mother and I think she refused to leave Jefferson's grave. Do you do that with someone you hate? Do you do that with somebody who forced you to be with him? I don't know if that's love or not, but it certainly speaks to me of commitment.

What people have to remember is that it was an illegitimate relationship, not only because of color, but because there were no ties of marriage. There's a stigma of illegitimacy for my whole family from the get-go. Being acknowledged as descendants somehow takes the sting away. It doesn't right a wrong, but it makes it okay. It's one thing to be illegitimate and accepted. It's another thing to be illegitimate and denied. It's like you have two strikes against you already.

Now the whole relationship is being held up to scrutiny. This is about a family. It's not a vehicle to make a political statement or headline stories or any of that other stuff. I think that if people are going to get bogged down in these personal agendas and try to make this into a media frenzy, it's really going to cheapen the story of the family. Family is where the heart is. Family is something that you extend to people. It's not just a word, it's a behavior. It's the way you treat people. It's the way people feel when they're around you.

I wanted to visit Monticello again—without the media there. So I returned and met with Dan Jordan, the president of the Thomas Jefferson Memorial Foundation, to see how recent events have changed life there. The Thomas Jefferson Memorial Foundation owns and operates Monticello. The memorial foundation is a private nonprofit organization and has no official connection with the Monticello Association, which owns and operates the family graveyard. On January 27, 2000, after over a year of extensive research—subsequent to the DNA findings—the Thomas Jefferson Memorial Foundation announced that, according to its research, Thomas Jefferson probably fathered one, if not all, of Sally Hemings's children.

Dan Jordan

THE RESPONSE TO OUR ANNOUNCEMENT HAS BEEN FAIRLY MODEST compared with the reaction to the DNA study. A relatively small number of people bothered to share their views, and most have been supportive. Some have been critical, and from a number of different angles. Some critics, we think, are just unstable personalities. They use ugly language and a vitriolic tone, and they seem to be conspiracy-minded. They think this was a plot by the British government to embarrass Jefferson because the British have never accepted the Declaration of Independence; or it's somehow or other connected to President Clinton's legacy. But we've also received some reasoned criticism, and we welcome that. In fact, we hope the report will be the beginning of a whole new round of serious research.

In my personal and professional opinion, this issue will not diminish Jefferson's legacy or importance to the American people. This new evidence, I believe, will help people to understand him. At last May's press conference, we used the cliché: "Whoever said history is dull?" At our most recent press conference, we used another cliché: "History is never over." As long as there's active research and good scholarship, history should be generating new information and new insights. The goal is to understand—not to defend and certainly not to denounce—a remarkable person and his times.

Just as the announcement was made to the press, we posted the report on the Internet. Within the first week after the press conference—in that seven days—3,000 different individuals downloaded the report, and the number of "hits" we were receiving came to about 60,000 a day. Two weeks later, in the wake of the CBS miniseries *Sally Hemings: An American Scandal,* the hits maxed out our system, and we had as many as 900,000 viewers in one day. Our Web master said that we had 3.3 million hits in one week!

We thought the movie was ridiculous as history—that it was a soap opera, that it was strictly Hollywood—but it certainly did encourage an interest in the story. Anything that encourages and raises the consciousness of the American people about history and race is a good thing. If some of the movie's audience comes for a tour of Monticello, we'll be responsive to their questions. Monticello has some wonderful tour guides, who are thoroughly trained, and we have great confidence in them. We have no scripts, either, so every tour should be a little different. If the guides are dealing with schoolkids, there will be a slightly different tour than if they are dealing with a group of architects, for example.

One thing I really resent, and this is a personal opinion, is being told that we're doing this just to be politically correct. I was trained as a scholar and a historian, and I've always believed that if you want something to be accurate, it has to be inclusive. You can't pick and choose and tell only part of a story. At Monticello, scholarship drives the mission. We have nine Ph.D.s on the staff and six colleagues who have published one or more books with a university press. On any given day, fifteen to twenty research projects are in motion. One of our scholars,

Cinder Stanton, is now completing a major book on the African-American families of Monticello. It examines documents, oral traditions, archaeology, and everything that's come from twenty years of analysis of the extraordinary families who lived and worked at Monticello. We hope this book will enable people to understand better not only Monticello and Jefferson but also the very complicated world of American slavery.

Monticello's African-American community has been a long-standing interest of ours. Through the Getting Word Oral History Project, we have interviewed over one hundred descendants of Jefferson's slaves. On the archaeological front, we have just received a major grant from the Mellon Foundation that will enable us to catalog, digitize, and share all of our plantation artifacts, which have been gathered from over twenty years of excavations. Another grant will enable us to assess restoring Mulberry Row, the main plantation street. We've published books; done a special pamphlet; sponsored lectures, conferences, and exhibits; and hosted several homecomings of the descendants of Jefferson's slaves.

Finding and restoring the Monticello slave burial grounds has also been of interest to us for many years. We made a concerted effort a few years ago, using the best technology of the National Park Service, and essentially came up empty-handed. Unfortunately, and amazingly, there is no clear documentation about where the burial sites are. The best prospect—the one that we investigated five or six years ago—will be investigated again this spring with more sophisticated equipment than was available to us a few years ago. We're keeping our fingers crossed as that work continues.

Although the foundation has no official connection with the Monticello Association, we do have a good working relationship with them, as we do with the Woodson Family Association and lots of other groups that have a vested interest in the Jefferson/Hemings issue. The Monticello Association told us that they would take very seriously our recently published research report, and it's our understanding that they intend to mail it out to each of their seven hundred dues-paying members. We see that as a very positive step. But it's hard to predict what will happen.

What we do know for sure is that the best way to connect with people is through a story. Often, the most powerful story is the one that's about your own family. Everybody has a family and everybody has a family story. I think young people would find it not only fascinating and rewarding but also a lot of fun to learn more about their family histories.

Getting Word

The Getting Word Oral History Project is a vital part of Monticello today. Its mission is to unearth and record the histories of the many African-American families that lived and worked at Monticello. Dedicated historians Lucia Stanton and Dianne Swann-Wright (pictured above), along with consultant Beverly Gray, collect documents and photographs and record interviews with descendants in order to preserve the oral history of these families. In doing so, they hope to contribute to an expanded and more balanced interpretation of the complex community—both black and white—that was Monticello.

Since most slaves could neither read nor write, oral communication was their primary way of knowing. They sought to "get word" of family members—from whom they had often been separated—and of events in the lives of those they cared about. The Monticello oral history project grew out of a recognition of the importance of oral traditions and their preservation.

The graveyard at Monticello is the source of the controversy, not the house and land. Two of the people debating the issue are Robert Golden, who is the current president of the Woodson Association, and James Truscott, the current president of the Monticello Association. Because they both live in the Pittsburgh area, I asked them if they would consider meeting together with me. This was the first time the two gentlemen had sat down and spoken. Both welcomed the opportunity, and I was glad to have had the opportunity to start a dialogue.

Robert Golden
& James Truscott

GOLDEN: In 1976, at the first Woodson reunion, 130 people came from all over the country. Many were people we didn't know, but they all shared the same oral history. The same identical oral history. I don't care what the DNA tests say, you could never convince me otherwise. It's impossible to convince me otherwise.

TRUSCOTT: I accept that. You believe that to be true. Quite likely it is true.

SHANNON: I do believe that Thomas Jefferson would want us to go forward in history, and that this generation wants the truth. Who knows what it could lead to? It could lead to the end of racism. This is the symbolism of our so-called first family. If we can be unified, why can't everyone else?

TRUSCOTT: That's a very important point. The difficulty with that is that it really doesn't have anything to do with determining the propriety of admitting Hemings descendants to the association. It would be a tremendous benefit, I believe, to the country to decide, "Okay, that's all good, and let's do it."

GOLDEN: You have to stop and think that the Hemingses built the cemetery.

They cleared the whole property there. They built that house and the whole property. That's what they did. And so that should certainly be reason enough for them to be allowed to be buried there. As I said, I have no interest in being buried there myself, but I should have the *right* to.

TRUSCOTT: I don't have a problem with that, but the Monticello Association has to figure out what are the right standards, if that is the word to use.

GOLDEN: They have to think about the "rights," considering all the "wrongs" that they've done. With the past "wrongs," they have to think about the "rights." What would be the *right* thing for them to do considering all the *wrong* they have already done? When you're talking to them about that, don't forget to raise that point. They brought us here in chains, beat us, paid us absolutely nothing. They got everything. We got nothing. Talk about equal opportunity!

Bob Golden holds a Woodson family daguerreotype of
his great-grandparents James Woodson and Anna Bird Moles.

SHANNON: What portion of the oral history weighs into the decision-making process?

TRUSCOTT: Right now, oral histories are a factor. I would say the Woodson oral histories are among the best—if not *the* best—in this situation. The DNA testing is another factor. The historical analysis—time and place—is another factor. How certain can we be from a historical study that Thomas Jefferson was at the right time and right place for Sally's children to be conceived? There are probably some genealogical issues that we'd better be looking at to try to pull all this together into a coherent bundle out of which we'll say, "Okay, it's clear now what all this means." So your question is: "What do the oral histories mean?" I think they may very well be a big factor, but I don't know that yet.

GOLDEN: They would have to be a big factor in order to be fair because there was nothing else that the slaves had. It was against the law to read and write. It was against the law to go to church. They had no rights, no benefits. Nothing at all. No marriage certificate. No certificate of birth for your child.

SHANNON: Even written facts can be changed. Who's to say that a person's father is his real one?

TRUSCOTT: I wouldn't doubt that we have members in the association who are not descendants. I suspect there are very few, but I wouldn't doubt it for a minute. The obvious case would be an adopted child. Someone adopts a child and they send their name in and say, "I have a new child." Well, the thing that made me mad about my nephew Lucian was that he said one thing that was absolutely untrue. He said that he could register his cat as a member, and that's just absolute hogwash. If you're a member of the association, you're a lineal descendant of Thomas Jefferson and, by definition, you're authorized to be buried in the graveyard. As I understand it, you must be a descendant of Thomas Jefferson to be buried in the bigger part of the graveyard. In the smaller part, you've got to be a descendant of Thomas Jefferson Randolph, Thomas's grandson. To conserve space in the graveyard, right now we're encouraging cremation. We encourage modest tombstones. We would not allow another obelisk.

GOLDEN: What I understand from some of the people in the Thomas Jefferson Memorial Foundation is that there are two or three slave cemeteries as well on the property, and nobody, so far, is certain where they are. *USA Today* also did some research and thinks that Sally Hemings is most probably buried under a Hampton Inn parking lot in downtown Charlottesville. I'd like to see the descendants of all the slaves who built Monticello have the right to be buried in the cemetery if they so desire—any of the descendants of any of the slaves who worked and built that place, although I don't know why they'd want to be.

Well, the ball is in the association's court now. They've got the opportunity to really give the country something it needs.

*T*here's actually a person who cares full time for the graveyard. She is Joy Rotch Boissevain, a sixth-generation descendant of Thomas Jefferson's daughter Martha. Joy was appointed to the position of keeper of the family graveyard when her mother retired. Joy serves on the Membership Advisory Committee recently assembled by the Monticello Association to study the current conflict over burial rights and to set up criteria for resolution. Professionally, Joy works for the University of Virginia's Center for the Study of Mind and Human Interaction, a group of psychoanalysts, diplomats, historians, political scientists, and others all working together to study conflict among people. Joy explained to me that sometimes focusing on people's commonalities can actually be dangerous.

Joy Rotch Boissevain

WHEN YOU HAVE TWO GROUPS THAT ARE NEIGHBORS, whether they're Turks and Greeks or Russians and Estonians, blacks and whites or Arabs and Jews, there are certain dynamics, rituals, and processes that happen at the large-group level. One thing that is quite clear is that if you try to push two groups together by pointing out their similarities, say, in their folk customs or their joint history, if you try to say that they are really the same, what you might actually do is push the two groups farther apart. It's sort of automatic and unconscious, as in the case of telling an Arab and a Jew that they both descend from Abraham. People need to maintain their differences because these differences are part of their identity. When people feel that their identity is threatened, they instinctively act to defend it. So you have to make sure there is a border between groups that is stable but also permeable so you don't have real conflict. I can imagine how, at the May 15, 1999, reunion weekend, anxiety levels were automatically high amongst both the Jefferson and Hemings descendants, because we're talking about crossing that border.

My grandfather Walter M. Whitehill was a historian. As a child I grew up revering him and hearing him and other family members deny the possibility of

Joy with her husband, Fitz, and son, Jeremy.

Thomas Jefferson and Sally Hemings's relationship. As is the case with the Hemingses and their oral history, I never questioned what our family told us. Quite honestly, I didn't think about it very much. People in my family said it wasn't true, so it just wasn't true.

I remember when Fawn Brodie's book *Thomas Jefferson: An Intimate History* came out in the seventies. I remember my grandfather and his colleagues criticizing Brodie's method of gathering information and interpreting it. I haven't read her book, but I've been rereading Annette Gordon-Reed's book *Thomas Jefferson and Sally Hemings: An American Controversy.* My overall impression is how helpful and amazingly impressive it is, taking apart piece by piece the different decisions and judgments made by historians. It is fascinating to me, because I can see how my grandfather and his colleagues just kind of built on what they wanted to believe. They weren't doing it dishonestly, but I also don't agree with what they did. I don't think we're ever going to know 100 percent what really happened between Jefferson and Hemings. I wish we could, because we can never completely settle the arguments, but I'm now convinced that there was a relationship.

There are those who say that you have to have legal proof, that you have to be able to prove it in the courts—and this is true, particularly when you talk about the graveyard, where there is a legal deed restriction involved. But part of me wants to say that slavery was legal first. There is no possibility of having a legal document, because Jefferson and Hemings could not have been married. How can you have legal proof? Don't you have to take that into consideration when you're trying to figure out what evidence is enough?

The idea that Thomas Jefferson and Sally Hemings may have had a sexual relationship provokes passionate denials from some people, yet the idea that he owned and sold slaves—that's been there all the time. The outrage at that has sort of stabilized. You can point to all sorts of contradictions. It's fascinating to hear that Jefferson sold one of his slaves to a neighbor because the slave and the neighbor were in love, and the slave couldn't go and live with the neighbor unless Jefferson sold her to him. To me this shows that they were working within a system that we can't quite get our minds around. I mean, Sally was Jefferson's wife's half sister. I didn't realize that until not that long ago.

The idea of Hemings and Jefferson descendants being together as a group in no way bothers me. I think that's because I don't think of the Jefferson heritage as sacrosanct, something to be protected. The words used by those who object are that we must protect the image and character and reputation of Thomas Jefferson, and that this somehow destroys it. Some think that if you're tearing down Jefferson, you're tearing down the foundations of this country. Some want to defend him against being called a hypocrite. If you see it that way, it builds it into a much stronger issue. But really, I think these are all defenses against not wanting to be mixed. If you see black people as not like you, you're never going to want to be part of the same group or family.

I think it's wonderful that Hemings and Jefferson descendants could be buried together. Of course, I'm not at any risk to my person to say this. I may be at risk of criticism from people who disagree with me, but I'm living in a time when it's really quite easy for me to say this. I don't know what I would say if I were asked to put my life, my reputation, my money, or my family on the line, as I believe they would have been years ago.

The Monticello Association is an organization that's now being put in the spotlight. Right now, all it's getting is attacked. But the things that are being asked of this little family association are bigger than anything it's ever had to do before. In the past, its most important concerns have been repairing the graveyard fence and where to go to dinner on Saturday night at the annual meeting.

Even within nuclear families you can find many different points of view, as is the case with Eston descendants Mary Jefferson and her sons, Colby and Justin Boggs. It was their cousin John Jefferson who provided the blood link in Dr. Foster's DNA study.

Mary Jefferson with sons, Colby & Justin

JUSTIN: I was raised knowing that I was English, Italian, Native American, and maybe a little more here and there. But I had no idea that I had African-American blood in me. I think that's cool! It's a good feeling to know where you come from. Some people think you're part of a specific family, but now I realize that we're all related. We're all part of each other's family. The white families are part of the black families, and the black families are part of the white families. There is no separate family. People are starting to figure that out, and I think it's good. It's good for this country.

MARY: Whether someone believes in creationism or evolution, we came from the same source.

COLBY: Yeah, it brings to light the sides of our history that have been swept under the rug. I think we're maturing a lot as a nation, with this new evidence that we're related. I think it's a big step forward.

JUSTIN: People are

realizing that American history is not exclusively a white history. There are a lot of things that went on that weren't recorded. What we're finding out now will change the way we view our history and ourselves.

MARY: I really think this is an exciting time for our country to discuss lineage and our heritage. We can be proud of wherever we come from. As a teacher and a public speaker, I've talked with students and staff members about their multiracial backgrounds and seen how excited they are to talk about it. It validates who they are. They talk about how having siblings of different colors has affected their lives. It's opened up dialogues that have been very healthy.

Growing up, I was interested in getting to know all kinds of people. In high school, I was involved in student exchange programs, in which we visited other schools that were unlike ours—they were Jewish or black, etc. And that was before I became aware of who I come from, and how this is so personal to me. I've always been interested in diversity and living in a diverse community. That's one of the reasons I left a certain city when Colby was a year old. We lived in a community where they had an unwritten law of no blacks after dark. Since I didn't want to raise my little baby in that kind of environment, I left the area.

COLBY: Thanks, Mom!

MARY: When I teach my students, I never put them into categories. My job is to encourage my students to find out about their heritage, because it makes life richer to have your heritage as part of your life rather than just saying, "Okay, I'm an American. I'm into macaroni and cheese." I think it's diversity that makes life interesting. That's why I reject the whole notion of the melting pot, because it makes us become one big mush. I prefer the quilt analogy, that each has his or her own part to contribute, parts that can retain their own identity and beauty yet be a part of the whole picture of what it is to be an American.

I know this because my mother was Italian, and at one point—like many others in her generation—she wanted to be very American. She never passed on her language to me, so I've lost out on that part of my heritage and I feel cheated. We've also been cheated by not knowing our black heritage. I'm envious of the stories and the pictures that my Hemings cousins have, and the history that they've known for so long. They really know who they are, and I think that helps solidify their self-awareness. Our link to Jefferson is supposed to be strong, because we have the DNA match, but we don't have the oral history. We're not really sure when the story was buried. We don't know whether it was when Eston added Jefferson to his last name and registered as white. We're not even sure whether his son Beverly knew he was black. We have a lot of dead ends in our family tree where people in the family did not get married, or if they did marry, they didn't have children. We've wondered if this was because they thought that they might have a black baby and be out of a career or a neighborhood or whatever. We have only fourteen living descendants of Eston, as compared to the Thomas Woodson branch, which has fifteen hundred!

COLBY: I think the lack of information on the Eston side of our family is unfortunate. But we're all proud of who we are and who our families are. I got the opportunity to meet more of my family when my mom convinced my brother, Justin, and me to attend the Monticello reunion. It was wonderful meeting relatives from all over the fifty states.

JUSTIN: Yeah, I think being there in '99 was very significant, but it would be interesting to go back again and have the association see that we're not going to disappear, and things can't go back to the way they were. If we keep going year after year, maybe they will recognize that we are descendants, too.

COLBY: I don't want to push myself into a group of people that doesn't want me. I'm proud of who I am, and, after finding out who my family is, I'm extremely proud. I honestly don't care what the association thinks. The evidence is there. They can choose to believe it or not.

I have no intention of being a part of the Monticello Association. I don't want to be married there, and I don't want to be buried there, so I don't feel that I need to go back. What I do need to do is to make contacts with my new family. I think that's the main goal for me, to make contact with my extended family. Besides, I love having an enlarged Christmas-card list!

MARY: I think for us not to go back to the Monticello Association's meetings is giving up too easily. It's like when women started pushing into the workplace and into men's organizations. They had to make a stand for something they believed in. I think this is the same kind of thing with the Monticello Association. I think we need to be strong, unified, and proud. The truth will win out, and we will then become members. Whether we want to be buried there is not the issue. We have a right to be there because we are descendants of Sally Hemings and Thomas Jefferson. It's a way to honor Sally's memory.

It was Nina in Atlanta who suggested that I talk with Ms. Roberts, her third cousin, and I'm very grateful for the suggestion. I've never had the pleasure of meeting Gloria Roberts in person because she lives in Munich, Germany. Although I would have loved to go to Europe for this interview, I had to do the next best thing and talk to her on the phone. A graduate of the Juilliard School of Music, she is a renowned concert pianist who has performed all over the world. One of the reasons Nina felt so strongly about my speaking to her cousin is because Ms. Roberts grew up in the same household as Madison Hemings's daughter, Ellen. Ellen was Ms. Roberts's grandmother.

Gloria Roberts

A youthful portrait of Gloria Roberts.

MY FATHER WAS FREDERICK MADISON ROBERTS. In 1919, he was the first African American elected to the California legislature. In fact, he was the first black officeholder elected west of the Mississippi after Reconstruction. During his sixteen years in office, he authored the state's first civil rights law, including laws dealing with discrimination in public schools. He was especially interested in protecting children. My father was also the first black male to graduate from Los Angeles High School. He was a director of the NAACP, YMCA, Urban League, and a trustee of the First AME Church.

In the legislature, my father was known as the Dean of the Assembly. His fellow members thought very highly of him because he was always fair and considered all sides. He was so fair-minded that he wouldn't even let my sister, Patricia, and me vote for him without reading up on the other candidates first.

You have to remember that when my father was in political office, the racial situation was not what it is today. California was not the South. We weren't segregated by laws or posted signs, but still we were segregated. It was more subtle; you could sit in a restaurant and simply be ignored.

Since my father was in the legislature, he was gone a lot of the time, but I was never alone. I lived in a big household, which included my mother and father, my father's sister Aunt Essie, her husband, Ivan Saunders, and, most importantly, my grandmother Ellen Wayles Hemings, who I called Grandmama. We all lived above the family mortuary, which was the first black mortuary in Los Angeles.

In our house, we all ate together, and Grandmama did all of the cooking. She did all the cleaning and washing, too. Aunt Essie was allowed to dust. But I can remember Grandmama fussing that Aunt Essie didn't dust well. We all lived together up until I was about nine years old. There were no children in the immediate neighborhood for me to play with, but thank goodness there was always Grandmama. She was my best friend, and my biggest playmate. I spent most of my time with her. Grandmama did not go places. She was home all the time. She knitted a lot and made many quilts. So I would sit on my little stool with a piece of string, and she showed me how to knit. Although Grandmama and I played a lot, we didn't do much talking. She just didn't talk much.

My grandmama was the daughter of Madison Hemings, which made her the granddaughter of Thomas Jefferson and Sally Hemings. Of course, she didn't talk about that, either. I always knew about Jefferson. I don't know how old I was when I was first told, but I always knew. I was told, "Oh, we just don't talk about it. Don't go around telling people." And because I was a good little girl, I didn't.

My mother said after she read Fawn Brodie's book *Thomas Jefferson: An Intimate History*, that that was the first time she realized where my father's middle name, Madison, came from—after his mother's father. She knew where our heritage came from—my father had told her—but she hadn't thought about it much. He told her: We don't talk about this. And to think all those years we never asked Grandmama about her father or anything! I should have asked her. She and her husband moved to Los Angeles from Ohio. My father was born in Chillicothe, Ohio. And I'm just so sorry that I didn't ask him things about his family. I'm sure he would have talked to Grandmama a lot about where she came from, her father, and so forth. What he didn't learn from her, he would have tried to track down.

I know Grandmama said they lost a lot of things in a house fire, things that were from Madison. But the family still has a few of those things. One of them is what I always remembered was called the "cranberry dish," because Grandmama always made fresh cranberry sauce for Thanksgiving and Christmas, and she always used this dish for that. It is a white glass bowl, with a painted red border, kind of worn. Not that we can specifically quote, but we know these treasures belonged to Grandmama, and we think that possibly they could have been given to her by Madison. They may have come from the Jefferson household.

My cousin Nelly Johnson Jones also had a pair of eyeglasses, and pen and inkwell, from Jefferson. Those, unfortunately, have disappeared. But Cousin Nell, as we called her, came to Los Angeles when I was young and brought those things. I had Jefferson's glasses on, I held his pen, and I was very put out with my family, because I wanted them to put some ink in the inkwell so I could really write, and they wouldn't do it. I thought, "Oh, this is from an older granddaddy. He's dead and gone. I didn't know that granddaddy," but I did know he was the President of the United States. And I thought, "Oh, my! Maybe he had these glasses on and used this pen when he was writing all those important things."

I knew that this older granddaddy was important, but I didn't have to have Jefferson to make me feel, "Oh there's somebody in my family that has accomplished something." Because when I was growing up, I had my father, and he was a big, important person right here in our community, and in the whole state of California.

We spoke of things then and over the years, and sometimes something would come up and we'd say, "Oh, that's a family trait." For instance, my father would play his violin, and we'd say, "Well, he got that from Jefferson. Jefferson played the violin." And then, Daddy being in politics, "Well, that runs in the family." And when we were broke, we'd say, "Oh, that runs in the family, too." Because, of course, Jefferson died bankrupt.

My family also inherited other traits from Jefferson. My grandmama was as white as she could be, with light, bright blue eyes, and her hair was white when I knew her. Jean Harlow was a big movie star at that time, and I thought Grandmama was a platinum blonde like her. But one day Grandmama was bending over, and I saw some dark hairs just at the nape of the neck, and, oh, that frightened me! I ran to tell Aunt Essie, "Something's wrong with Grandmama!" and Aunt Essie said, "Well, it's just her dark red hair," and she assured me that it was okay. Grandmama had been a redheaded young woman, dark red. Another Jefferson trait.

I might say, too, as a youngster, race was never mentioned in our family. We didn't talk about race. Even as a child I might speak of a brown person, dark brown person, a white person, but I was describing the way they looked. In my immediate family, as I said before, Grandmama was white as could be. Aunt Essie was light brown. My father was a little bit medium brown. My mother was fair, kind of Mexican-looking, but not really. Aunt Essie's husband, Uncle Ivan, was dark brown. And then there was me. I'm kind of light brown. My eyes are greenish gray, and my hair is also red. So in my immediate family, those that I saw every day, I had all different shades of color around me.

People were different colors, and I didn't think about that until I started school. That's when I finally found out there were white people. Oh, the tears and the fusses through school. Back in those days, we were colored or Negro, and you would have school papers that would indicate where you were born, your nationality, and your race.

My father told me, if anybody asked you what you are, tell them, "You're an American." If they keep probing, well, tell them you're an "American of African descent." So if I had put "Negro" down on my papers, my father would scratch it out and make me put "American of African descent." Once my father even wrote "purple" over what I had written. And I said, "Oh, Daddy, I can't take that back to school!" Then one day he got the dictionary out, and we looked up the word "Negro," and he said, "You read what a Negro is." They described somebody with black skin and white, bulging, yellowish eyes and big protruding lips and a flat nose and whatnot, and my dad said, "Does that describe you?" I was shocked at what I read, so I replied, "Why, no!" He said, "Then why do you want to put down 'Negro' and say that that's what you are?" From then on, I proudly put down "American."

Although I've been living in Europe since 1964, I'm still an American citizen, and I wouldn't change that for anything in the world. Absolutely not. I'm

Ellen Wayles Hemings, granddaughter of Thomas Jefferson (top). *Frederick Roberts, her son and Gloria's father* (bottom).

very proud to be an American. There are many things about America that upset me, but still we have made great progress in righting some wrongs. We still have a lot to do, but I'm the person I am today because I'm able to understand and take in different cultures. And I'm able to do that because of how I was brought up, and the opportunities that were available to me in the U.S.A.

As an American, I still take my responsibility to vote very seriously. Even though I currently reside in Europe, I always get an absentee ballot. I've often wondered if they ever notice how much I've been absent! The last time I was filling out an absentee form, and I got to the place where you fill in nationality and race, and I thought, "What? I thought we didn't have those things anymore!" So I just filled in "American" and left the rest blank.

As an American, I feel that, little by little, the love story of Thomas Jefferson and Sally Hemings will be completely accepted. I do think of it as a true love story. Sometimes a man and a woman are just meant for each other. They were victims of their time. I know a lot of people feel he was two-faced, that he said one thing and did another. But he must have had great torturous thoughts. I think he truly believed, as he wrote, that all men are created equal, but here he is. He was a product and a prisoner of his time. People have slaves, so he has slaves. What is he going to do? Yes, he can give up all the slaves, and he and Sally can do what? How is he going to make a living? Where are they going to go? They were not allowed to live together by law, and if she were free, she would have had to have left Virginia within a year. The country and we, today, would have lost a lot of great things he did and all he had to offer.

I feel that they were caught up in the morals and culture of the times, but that they stayed together the best they could. And when I look back at my family's rich heritage and the legacy they left, I'm grateful that they stayed together—and we all should be.

Like Gloria Roberts, my great-aunt Jackie and Mrs. Jerry Woodson believe that it was a true love story between Thomas and Sally, and that their children were products of that love. Mrs. Woodson and my aunt met each other for the first time at our family campout in 1999, but it seemed as if they had always known each other. Their husbands have both recently passed on, but they still proudly uphold the Hemings oral history that comes through their husbands' families. They believe that love is the single most important thing in our family, as I clearly witnessed watching them surrounded by their children and grandchildren that weekend. It is their belief that someday people everywhere will come to experience love for each other, as we do in our family.

Jackie Pettiford & Jerry Woodson

MRS. WOODSON: On my side of the family, I had an Aunt Sarah. She lived in Jeffersonville, Ohio, and she had been a slave. We used to go ask her to tell stories about the old times. She could sit and tell all kinds of things that happened back in slavery days. But, you know, she never hated anybody. She had a right to, but she *didn't*.

GREAT-AUNT JACKIE: They didn't, thank God. They sang spirituals and—

MRS. WOODSON: They had more than hate—they had God and they had love for one another. You don't know what's in your family.

GREAT-AUNT JACKIE: All we knew when Jack and I got married was that we were related to Thomas Jefferson. Aunt Mae would say, "Do you know that Thomas Jefferson was your grandfather?" Well, we laughed about it and thought it was funny. There was no documentation that we knew of then; we didn't have anything in writing. But Jack was real interested in it once it all started coming together, and he did a lot of research with our niece Patti Jo in Chillicothe.

MRS. WOODSON: We knew that Thomas Jefferson bought a farm down in Jackson, Ohio, and sent his slave there, changed his name to Woodson. And on my

Jerry and Jackie (top).

Jackie with granddaughter Georgia (right).

side, my great-great-grandfather—who was a minister—performed the Woodson boy's wedding.

GREAT-AUNT JACKIE: Jefferson bought some property in Ross County, too, where Madison lived. There was an article in our paper not too long ago about a farmer whose grandfather used to tell him stories about Madison being on the farm next to him. He said Madison looked just like Jefferson. They called him Little Tom and said he looked just like him.

MRS. WOODSON: You know, that's why I'm just so happy that Sally told her children that Thomas Woodson was her son, and that it was brought out as the truth. If you stop and think about all our kids that are descendants of Thomas Jefferson, if they were true black people, they would not be those white colors. They would not have the hair. They would not have the features. None of my husband's family looks black. They all look white, every one of them. They all look white, redheads and blondes.

GREAT-AUNT JACKIE: I heard a man on TV say, "If anyone ever had slavery in their family two hundred or three hundred years ago, you've got black relatives and you've got black blood somewhere in your family." Of course, any time I say I'm black, people want to know, "Which one of your parents is black?" My parents were both black. My grandparents were black. We were always told that we were black, and we came up as black. My mother was fairer than I am, and I never paid it any attention. It wasn't an issue as to what shade you were. Her grandfather had been a product of a slave and a white man. He had blond hair and blue eyes.

MRS. WOODSON: We have everything in us. We have Indian in us, we have white in us; my husband even had Jewish in him. It got so bad for my husband, Jim, that when he was in the service, they asked him what his race was. He said, "Why, I'm black." But on his discharge it read: Caucasian. They thought he was joking! They refused to accept him as being black.

GREAT-AUNT JACKIE: My husband, Jack, had that same problem when he went into the service. He said, "I'm black, I'm colored." And they kept arguing with him. He said, "I know what I am!" It makes no difference what we are. There is no pure anything. We have been mixing since biblical times. We need to get past this, and when we believe that the same blood runs through all our bodies, we'll be so much better off. Many years ago, *"that one ounce of blood"* made you black, so you didn't venture too far from your own color. No matter what you looked like, you still had to marry black. But my momma raised us so that we married whoever we fell in love with. There's never been any word as to who was white or black. We were taught to love everyone. We never even thought about race. So I raised my kids the same way. Some of my kids are married to black, and some of them are married to white. I just say, they can be anything they want to be. Just be good people. Just be what you want to be and do right in the world.

MRS. WOODSON: That's the way Jim and I raised our children, too. Two of our sons are married to white girls, and my grandchildren are gorgeous. Every time I see one of our children go off and I see them come back with their families, all different colors, it makes me so happy. Because I think this is the way it's supposed to be. Yes. This is the way it's supposed to be. This is God's plan.

As I neared the end of my journey, I felt it was important to get the views of the next generation. Our elders' belief that one day we will all be one family is shared by my eleven-year-old cousin Hunter Nobles. Hunter attended the Monticello Association meeting with his mom and dad, Charlotte and Peter. They came all the way from California. Hunter's heroic voice was not one that you would have read about in the papers, but to me his courage and his belief in the truth were one of the most important stories there.

Charlotte & Hunter Nobles

CHARLOTTE: Growing up, we vaguely knew that we were descendants of Thomas Jefferson, through his daughter Martha. My mother made nothing of it. The only family that I ever knew was my immediate family. All of my mother's books, records, old diaries, and stuff were always away in boxes, and I never saw them, and so it was not a reality for me. But it's been different for my son, Hunter. We went to Monticello for the first time in May 1999 to bury my mother with her family in the Monticello graveyard.

It was a bittersweet weekend. While we were down there, we were told that this was also the weekend of the reunion for not only the members of the Jefferson family but also the Hemings family. This was the first time they'd been invited. We decided it was important to be there for that. So we went from our small private burial services to meeting all these people! I always liked the idea of a big family. That's what I wanted my son, Hunter, to experience, because it was so unlike what I had when I was little.

My mother was a very progressive and liberal-minded person. She was a social democratic type. She liked politics, and she was kind of vocal about it. To her, people were judged by what they did, not by how much money they had or what they looked like. So that's how I grew up, and that's how I raised my son. Closed-mindedness is something that's never been a part of our household.

My husband, Peter, and I had never attended an association meeting before, but this year we felt it was important to support our Hemings cousins. Hunter was so excited that he was going to have a chance to vote, but he couldn't believe what was going on. He thought the conflict between the Jeffersons and the Hemingses was ridiculous. He wanted to express his opinion, and his dad and I encouraged him to do that.

HUNTER: It was so unfair that the association was trying to make part of my new family leave the meeting, so I stood up to vote for them to stay. But then it was kind of weird, because they told me to sit down because I was too young to vote, and I was like, "Okay, fine." But I was actually kind of embarrassed that they made me sit down. The old-fogy people probably didn't want to listen to me because they only wanted their opinion to matter. But I think adults should listen to us more, because we're going to be the future soon and we have opinions, too.

I listen to my parents, and they tell me everything. They don't try to keep anything from me. They say, "It doesn't matter what color people are, you can still be a good friend to them, and you shouldn't fight people just because they look different than you." I think it doesn't matter what color you are, if you love a person, you just love the person. Like, I love my godmother, Shanda, and she's black. But when people see us walking down the street and we're hugging and stuff, sometimes they'll just stare at us. But then Shanda will say, "Oh, he's my son!" And we laugh, and the people are like, "Whoa!"

But I don't care how they feel. I don't mind it at all, because racism isn't going to be a problem in the future. No, not at all. I think our generation is going to get it right, because with everything that's happening in the world, it isn't going to last much longer. So I think we're going to kind of finally get it into our heads that we need to act together and not just as individuals. Because there are so many different people in the world and eventually we'll all learn that we're just fighting each other. I mean, we're all the same species and stuff, and just 'cause your skin color is different, and you look a little different, doesn't mean that you should hate each other. You have different beliefs, but it doesn't mean that you can't still be friends or anything. I think we're going to learn to get along with each other, and basically the whole world's going to unite. Maybe not in my lifetime, although I hope it is. I can't make any promises, but it'll be soon.

Oh, one more thing, we should all just get along. That's basically it.

An hour after my family—the Hemingses and Jeffersons—met for the first time on *Oprah*, they had a chance to sit down for a meal together without the whole nation watching. During this intimate and momentous occasion, my cousin, the Reverend Doug Banks, led our family in prayer. Spirituality is something that runs deeply in my family. Doug based his prayer on some of the ideas from Dr. King's "I Have a Dream" speech. I asked him what led him to think of this.

William Douglas Banks

IT JUST KIND OF DAWNED ON ME THAT DAY, with our family there together, that this was really what Dr. King was speaking of. He had dreamed of a day when this would happen, when "the sons of former slaves and the sons of former slave owners will be able to sit down together at the table of brotherhood." Forty years ago, people were only dreaming about it, and here it was happening in our family. It wasn't anything that I had prepared to say, it was just something that God had kind of showed me in that moment, and when I prayed I was just thankful to participate in that.

It's good to see when God gives us a vision of the future, and it's good to see when it comes to pass. Many times we don't appreciate what we've asked God to do.

What excited me about this experience of finding my newfound family is that it creates a larger sense of community, or at least the possibility for that, based upon a common heritage. I would like to use the word *diallosso*, when thinking about my family. *Diallosso* is a Greek word in the New Testament where Jesus says, "First go be reconciled with your brother." It's translated as "be reconciled," but it's the only word in the New Testament that denotes two parties coming to the table and creating a different new solution that benefits both of them. It's not domination, where one person gets his or her way and the other doesn't. Both parties input on it.

The reconciliation that takes place between humanity starts with two

Doug and his wife, Erica.

people. Two people sit down at the table and say, "Okay, let's squash this." That's what God calls for humanity to do, to be reconciled: *Diallosso.* "Y'all sit down and work this out." And that's something that few people really want to do. It's easy to just be mad at somebody all your life. It's hard to deal with it and come to the table. That's the hard work that we don't want to do, on an individual basis, within our own families, or on a national basis. Hopefully, this book will help facilitate those kinds of dialogues. They need to happen in order for change to take place.

*S*ometimes I reach into my pocket and find a nickel. Ever since I was very small there's been a quiet little game I've played. I look at the two sides of the coin and think about how they symbolize my family. On the face of the nickel is my great-grandfather Thomas Jefferson. On the other side is Monticello, the great house built by my family, the Hemingses, and the other slave families who lived at Monticello. Together they symbolize the two sides of my heritage and the enormous pride and strength both hold for me.

I have tremendous hope for my family. A year after first meeting my extended family—the day I first met Jane, and we began the journey that is now this book—I recall very tense circumstances at Monticello. At that first reunion, kids clung to their parents, who cautioned them about playing with the other kids. By the very next year, and as this book was getting ready to be published, I watched little Hemingses and little Jeffersons running around and playing together on the great lawn at Monticello, knowing each other now as cousins.

Yes, I have great hopes for this family—and for the greater extended family that is America. As with all families, communication is the key. We hope in some way the story of my family can inspire dialogue and communication in our greater American family. I urge everyone to take the journey that we have taken, to travel around and meet your family, to talk to your elders and hear their stories, to tap into the richness and variety that every American family holds and that we all have in common because we are, through our common history and our common blood, truly one American family.

The Jefferson Family

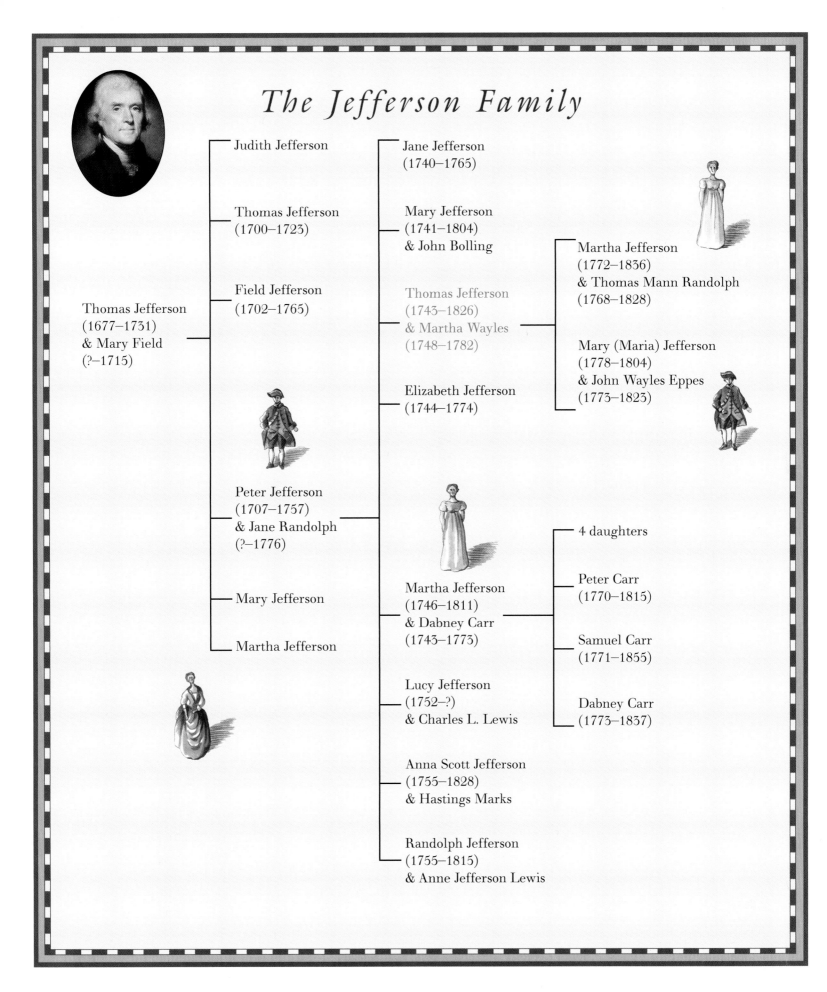

Thomas Jefferson
(1677–1731)
& Mary Field
(?–1715)

Judith Jefferson

Thomas Jefferson
(1700–1723)

Field Jefferson
(1702–1765)

Peter Jefferson
(1707–1757)
& Jane Randolph
(?–1776)

Mary Jefferson

Martha Jefferson

Jane Jefferson
(1740–1765)

Mary Jefferson
(1741–1804)
& John Bolling

Thomas Jefferson
(1743–1826)
& Martha Wayles
(1748–1782)

Elizabeth Jefferson
(1744–1774)

Martha Jefferson
(1746–1811)
& Dabney Carr
(1743–1773)

Lucy Jefferson
(1752–?)
& Charles L. Lewis

Anna Scott Jefferson
(1755–1828)
& Hastings Marks

Randolph Jefferson
(1755–1815)
& Anne Jefferson Lewis

Martha Jefferson
(1772–1836)
& Thomas Mann Randolph
(1768–1828)

Mary (Maria) Jefferson
(1778–1804)
& John Wayles Eppes
(1773–1823)

4 daughters

Peter Carr
(1770–1815)

Samuel Carr
(1771–1855)

Dabney Carr
(1773–1837)

The Hemings Family

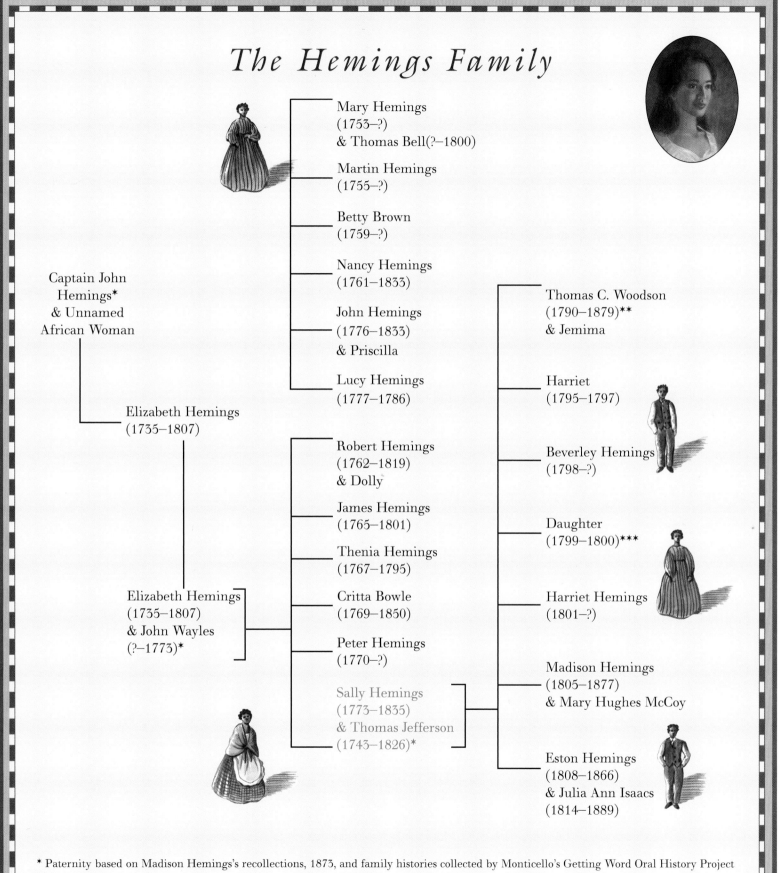

Captain John
Hemings*
& Unnamed
African Woman

Elizabeth Hemings
(1735–1807)

Mary Hemings
(1753–?)
& Thomas Bell(?–1800)

Martin Hemings
(1755–?)

Betty Brown
(1759–?)

Nancy Hemings
(1761–1833)

John Hemings
(1776–1833)
& Priscilla

Lucy Hemings
(1777–1786)

Elizabeth Hemings
(1735–1807)
& John Wayles
(?–1773)*

Robert Hemings
(1762–1819)
& Dolly

James Hemings
(1765–1801)

Thenia Hemings
(1767–1795)

Critta Bowle
(1769–1850)

Peter Hemings
(1770–?)

Sally Hemings
(1773–1835)
& Thomas Jefferson
(1743–1826)*

Thomas C. Woodson
(1790–1879)**
& Jemima

Harriet
(1795–1797)

Beverley Hemings
(1798–?)

Daughter
(1799–1800)***

Harriet Hemings
(1801–?)

Madison Hemings
(1805–1877)
& Mary Hughes McCoy

Eston Hemings
(1808–1866)
& Julia Ann Isaacs
(1814–1889)

* Paternity based on Madison Hemings's recollections, 1873, and family histories collected by Monticello's Getting Word Oral History Project
** Based on Woodson family oral history
*** Some debate exists as to when this girl, who lived only a year, was born

Acknowledgments

We would like to gratefully acknowledge the Divine forces that brought us together and stayed with us throughout this journey. We thank Oprah Winfrey for midwifing this book by first inviting members of both the Jefferson and the Hemings families to meet on her show, just ten days after the DNA results were published. To our nuclear and extended families, who not only shared much of themselves, their treasured ancestral photos, and their family stories but also gave us places to stay, fed us, and supported us in ways that cannot be put into words.

To Mary Hemmings for her faithful transcription work. To Dan Jordan and Whitney Espich at The Thomas Jefferson Memorial Foundation. To Cinder Stanton and Dianne Swann-Wright at the Getting Word Oral History Project. To Beverly Gray for her guidance, patience, and many contributions. To Lucian K. Truscott IV for his introductions, not only to this book but also to the many members of the family that have now met as a result of his invitation to Monticello. To the Monticello Association and its president, James Truscott. To the Woodson Association and its president, Robert Golden.

We would also like to acknowledge the vision of Kate Klimo and Craig Virden at Random House, who did not hesitate in making this book a reality. For Jim Thomas, our faithful and demanding editor. To Elizabeth Stevens for always being there for us—especially when we called in from the road with unusual requests. To Cathy Goldsmith, Jason Zamajtuk, Bob Antler, and Sallie Baldwin, our miracle-worker designers. To Judith Haut for her constant enthusiasm in promoting this book. To everyone else at Random House for their support.

To Tina Andrews, Ed Clay at WOSU Stations, and Robert Shapiro at Social Tees in NYC for the continued positive messages of his T-shirts. To Denise Gillman for her guidance. To Michelle McHugh. To Edgar Feldman for turning up the heat—and prompting Jane to first reach Lucian, in time to be invited to Monticello.

To the staff and students at Kent State University and the Hughes Center in Cincinnati for their continued interest in and support of all Shannon's endeavors. To our CityKids Foundation family—and particularly John Peralta, who, upon seeing the May 15, 1999, family photo at Monticello, hungered to learn more. To the Darrow School, which gave Jane an extraordinary educational foundation and an insatiable lifelong desire to learn. To the early *Life* photographers, Gordon Parks and others, who taught her about the power of image.

To Fawn Brodie for her courage in writing *Thomas Jefferson: An Intimate History* back in the early 1970s and her efforts to bring the family together for the first time. To Minnie Woodson for assembling *The Woodson Source Book*. To Annette Gordon-Reed for her invaluable contributions. To Patti Jo Harding and Ann and Jack Pettiford for their research, and for all those who contributed to this book. Finally, thank you to all those who kept the family's oral history alive!

p. 53: Art for DNA chart by Rodica Prato

p. 92–93: "Civil Rights Marchers Gather for Demonstration" photo: © Bettmann/CORBIS

p. 96–97: "Civil Rights Demonstrators in Selma, Alabama" photo: © Bettmann/CORBIS

p. 98: Anita Hemings portrait (within Jill Sim portrait): courtesy of Special Collections, Vassar College Libraries, Poughkeepsie, NY (class of 1897)

p. 98: Frederick Hemings portrait (within Jill Sim portrait): courtesy of Institute Archives and Special Collections, MIT Libraries, Cambridge, MA (senior portfolio, 1897)

p. 113: Dan Jordan photo: © Jen Fariello Photography (courtesy of Monticello/The Thomas Jefferson Memorial Foundation, Inc.)

p. 116: Monticello Graveyard plaque courtesy of the Monticello Association

p. 140–141: Art for Jefferson and Hemings family trees by Rodica Prato

p. 140–141: Jefferson and Hemings family trees: courtesy of Monticello/The Thomas Jefferson Memorial Foundation, Inc.

All other archival photos generously contributed to the book by the Hemings and Jefferson families
All other contemporary photos copyright © 1999–2000 Jane Feldman

For More Information...

BOOKS

Edward Ball, *Slaves in the Family* (Ballantine Books, 1998)

Edwin M. Betts, editor, *Thomas Jefferson's Farm Book* (University Press of Virginia, 1953, reprinted 1976)

Fawn M. Brodie, *Thomas Jefferson: An Intimate History* (W. W. Norton & Company, 1974)

Joseph J. Ellis, *American Sphinx: The Character of Thomas Jefferson* (Alfred A. Knopf, 1997)

Annette Gordon-Reed, *Thomas Jefferson and Sally Hemings: An American Controversy* (University Press of Virginia, 1997)

Jan Ellen Lewis and Peter J. Onuf, editors, *Sally Hemings and Thomas Jefferson: History, Memory, and Civic Culture* (University Press of Virginia, 1999)

Dumas Malone, *Jefferson and His Time*, 6 vols. (Little, Brown and Company, 1970)

William Safire, *Scandalmonger: A Novel* (Simon & Schuster, 2000)

Lucia C. Stanton, *Slavery at Monticello* (University Press of Virginia, 1996)

Mark Twain, *Pudd'nhead Wilson* (Bantam Classic Books, 1st edition 1894, Bantam 1959, Bantam Classic 1981)

Henry Wiencek, *The Hairstons: An American Family in Black and White* (St. Martin's Press, 1999)

Minnie S. Woodson, *The Woodson Source Book: From Utopia to the World*

FILMS

Sally Hemings: An American Scandal. Available on Hallmark Home Entertainment.
    Writer/co-producer Tina Andrews/Craig Anderson Productions/CBS Entertainment

Thomas Jefferson: A Film by Ken Burns www.pbs.org/jefferson

WEB SITES

Ancestors www.pbs.org/kbyu/ancestors/index.html

Ancestry.com www.ancestry.com

AQ Family Tree Research Center Online www.ancestralquest.com

A Conflict Resolution Page www.geocities.com/athens/8945

FamilySearch Internet Genealogy Service www.familysearch.org

Frontline www.pbs.org/wgbh/pages/frontline/shows/jefferson

Monticello (The Thomas Jefferson Memorial Foundation, Inc.) www.monticello.org

The Monticello Association www.monticello-assoc.org

Thomas C. Woodson Family Association www.woodson.org

Thomas Jefferson Online Resources at the University of Virginia http://etext.lib.virginia.edu/jefferson

The Thomas Jefferson Papers at the Library of Congress
    http://memory.loc.gov/ammem/mtjhtml/mtjhome.html

United States Institute of Peace www.usip.org

INDEX